DRAFTING SCENERY

DRAFTING SCENERY

for Theater, Film, and Television

Rich Rose

BETTERWAY PUBLICATIONS, INC.

WHITE HALL, VIRGINIA

Published by Betterway Publications, Inc.
P.O. Box 219
Crozet, VA 22932
(804) 823-5661

Cover design by Kayte Bullock
Typography by Typecasting

Library of Congress Cataloging-in-Publication Data

Rose, Rich
    Drafting scenery for theater, film, and television/
Rich Rose
        p.   cm.
    ISBN 1-55870-142-7: $22.95.
    ISBN 1-55870-141-9 (pbk.): $14.95.
    1. Theaters—Stage-setting and scenery.
2. Mechanical drawing. I. Title.
PN2091.S8R585   1990
    792′.02′921—dc20   89–18359
                                                            CIP

Printed in the United States of America
0 9 8 7 6 5 4 3 2 1

To Leslie

Acknowledgments

Thank you to all of the Draftspersons, Art Directors, and Designers who contributed so much to this book. I would especially like to thank Roy Christopher, Erin Dresel, Jo-anne McMaster, Greg Richman, Leslie Rose, Bruce Ryan, Brian Schindler, and Taki Shimojima for volunteering their outstanding examples of draftsperson's art.

Contents

Foreword

When I was asked to teach a class in drafting for the theater during my first year at UCLA, I immediately went about the business of preparing the course by researching the materials that I could use to teach drafting to beginning students of design and technical production. I thought back through the process that I had undergone in learning how to draft and realized that I had learned the techniques of drafting first in an architectural context and then, over a rather long and unorganized period of practical experience, learned to apply these techniques to the theater. This was neither a very effective nor an efficient model on which to base the course.

In teaching a course in drafting specifically for the theater, I wanted to develop a process that combined the common techniques and principles of drafting with the special language, problems, and requirements of the theater. It was at this point that a test copy of *Drafting Scenery* was made available to me. The material not only provided the basic outline of the course that I had imagined with a step-by-step process for learning to draft for the theater, but also an assortment of supplemental materials and examples. Here in one book was the vast majority of what I felt was necessary to provide a student with the basic understanding and techniques of drafting for the theater, film, and television.

Rich Rose provides a clear and concise course of study for drafting scenery. The text is organized in the same fashion as a well organized set of drawings. After preliminary discussions on such topics as the use of drafting tools and equipment, line types and weights, and lettering techniques; the book moves quickly to the foundation of all drawings, the ground plan. From this point, with the ground plan as reference, the text proceeds through the various types of drawings required in the theater from the basics of designer's elevations to the intricacies of perspective sketches. Each section includes a discussion of the nature of each type of drawing; the special techniques, graphic standards, and formats in current use by professionals; and a checklist of items to be included on that particular type of drawing. At the end of each section is a useful project, which illustrates the drawing in a hands-on fashion.

There are many distinctive features of this book. Outstanding are the numerous professional examples provided to illustrate the techniques and types of drawings required in the theater. Rich selects from his own extensive library to provide examples of nearly every conceivable variety. The use of these examples is not only illustrative in the context of the classroom, but also enables the students to see how the techniques they are learning are commonly applied by the professional. He also provides quality drawings in support of the text; illustrations of current graphic standards; and simple, easy to follow, step-by-step drawings to illustrate graphic solutions.

I have been using a test copy of this book for the past two years in both my drafting classes and as a recommended reference for students needing a refresher. My students have benefited tremendously from its use and perhaps have helped to create this published version. This book is just what I needed, and I am very pleased it is now available to all.

Thanks, Rich!

Daniel A. Ionazzi
Production Manager
Department of Theater
University of California, Los Angeles

Introduction

Drafting is an elemental and powerful skill that must be mastered by the scenic designer if he or she is to see the design successfully come to its full realization on stage. In a very real way it is another language that must be mastered in order to communicate with the many people responsible for carrying out all elements of the design. This is not unlike the musician who must understand the vocabulary of notes, sharps, flats, and rests in order to speak or read the language of music. The greatest composer is voiceless without the ability to communicate to each instrument in the orchestra. The greatest designer is powerless without the ability to articulate his or her conceptions in the language of scenography.

But oh that language! Anybody who tries to explain the language of scenic drafting is in for quite an assignment. For unlike architectural drafting, which has a vocabulary and a set of standards and conventions understood and followed by all architects, scenic drafting has long suffered from a lack of such uniformity. Just about every draftsperson you talk to has their own thoughts regarding the "right way" or "wrong way" to draft. The United States Institute for Theater Technology (USITT) has recently begun work on a standardization of drafting for both scenic and lighting design. For example, they have developed a template of standard lighting design symbols that they would like all lighting designers to use in drafting lighting plots. They have also begun to standardize terms and symbols in scenic drafting. Both of these efforts are meeting with mixed reaction and success. It is fairly difficult to change long standing methods and habits.

It's pretty clear that any book about scenic drafting cannot realistically be a book about the iron clad standards that are in place. For the most part there aren't any. This also isn't intended to be a book about what one person thinks these standards ought to be. Instead, *Drafting Scenery* is the result of many years of my own scenic drafting and reading the drafting of others. This book strives to describe the common threads that weave through most scenic drafting. When the book says, for example in the section on ELEVATIONS, that all titles in a drawing must be about a quarter inch high and underlined, it is because this is the way that most draftspersons deal with the issue. Conventions such as these are preferred not because there is a rule written anywhere, and not because it is my invention that I insist everyone follow. It is simply a fact that, nine times out of ten, the method pointed out in the book is the method that most draftspersons will use.

Drafting Scenery is divided into two parts. Each division could be the basis for a drafting course in itself. In the first part you will learn to draft a complete set of working drawings for a simple set. This will include learning about drafting equipment and gathering the tools you will need to begin. This first part will go on to introduce you to lettering, title blocks, using line weights, dimensioning, developing a floor plan, developing a more detailed platform plan, front and rear construction elevations, section views, detail views, and the center line vertical section. All of this will culminate in a project designed to test your newly developed drafting abilities in all of these basic skill areas.

The second part of the book will show you how to make your drawings clearer and more descriptive. Some issues that come up in more complicated drafting cannot be solved with the types of views explored in the first part. These assignments can only be addressed with some of the techniques covered in the later sections. The second half introduces you to the techniques designed to enrich your drafting. These areas include introducing textures and shading to your drawings, pictorial drawings (axonometric, oblique, and perspective views), and determining the true shape and true curve of certain foreshortened objects.

Together the two halves of *Drafting Scenery* will equip you with sufficient vocabulary to allow you to start communicating in the language of lines that is scenic drafting. You should never consider your education in scenic drafting complete. As new materials are introduced into scenic design and art direction with their own special techniques for use, they will influence the way that the drafting vocabulary evolves.

One More Note

By reading this book and successfully completing the exercises you should be able to fully draft a scenic design for production. That set of drawings goes by many names. You may be familiar with "the plans" or simply "the drawings." Sometimes these same drawings are referred to as "the blueprints," even though more and more the blueprint machine has been moved out and replaced with a large format photocopier. Other terms used are "working drawings," "construction drawings," and "shop drawings." The point is that whatever term you like, you use, or you hear, they are all acceptable and all mean the same thing. As you read on, you will notice most of these terms used interchangeably throughout the book.

1. Drafting Equipment

The draftsperson needs an assortment of precision tools to get the job done. When beginning your collection, you should shop around and buy only high quality name brand equipment that will serve you for many, many years. High quality equipment does not come too cheap, but this investment will actually save you money otherwise spent replacing broken tools in the years to come. Some of these quality brands include Pickett, Lighting Associates, Charvoz, Koh-I-Noor, Fuller, and Staedtler Mars.

Drafting Table

Of primary importance is a good drafting table. Many models and variations exist with price tags varying anywhere from about a hundred dollars on up into the thousands of dollars.

How do you choose a table?

1. Size has to be the first consideration. The table has to be big enough for the paper and your drafting equipment. If you're using 24″ × 36″ paper you will want to have a board that can accommodate the paper; extra space at the bottom of the table for the drafting machine arm, parallel, or T-square (4″–6″); and at least a foot of space on the right (or left if you are left handed) for your equipment. The result in this case is a 30″ × 46″ table. This space should be clear of a parallel or T-square which would otherwise be knocked to the floor with every pass. Some draftspersons prefer an *extra* table for all of their tools. A tabouret is just such a table with many slide-out and swing-out drawers.

The tabouret doubles as both an equipment table and a storage cabinet for the drafting tools. (Long-term storage of your large collection of drafting tools is also an important consideration for your drafting/design studio.)

2. All of these considerations must be balanced with the size of the room in which you are drafting. You will need room for your table, chair or stool, tabouret or other tool storage area, and plan storage area. Plan storage is usually done in large flat drawers called flat files. Another method uses a series of wall- or floor-mounted tubes which contain the rolled-up drawings.

3. Stability is an important factor when deciding upon a table. A table must be rock stable when performing functions such as drawing and erasing. If it is not, the quality of your presentation will suffer greatly. Although most tables sway a little, try to find one that keeps it to a minimum.

4. Flexibility may be important to you also. Most tables have some degree of height and tilt adjustment. The flexibility of these adjustments falls into two categories. First is the type that allows adjustment only after a great deal of work on your part with a couple of tools at hand. The second type allows adjustment with pneumatic, electric, and other types of controls which make adjusting the table quite effortless. If many people will be sharing the same table it will be important to have an easily adjustable table. If you plan to do other activities such as rendering or layout work that require different height and tilt adjustments, you may also want a high degree of flexibility. If you are going

to be the only one using your table and will be doing only drafting work, then a less flexible (and less expensive) table may suit your needs just fine. Don't buy a table with expensive "bells and whistles" you'll never use.

The Drafting Table Surface

The surface of the drafting table must be prepared prior to any drafting. The soft wood top of the drafting table makes for a terrible drawing surface that the pencil will sink right into. The top must be covered with a special rubberized material which provides just the right amount of flexibility for the pencil. Borco is a common brand but many others exist. The material comes on a roll and must be left to flatten out and shrink over a 24-hour period before it can be cut to size and attached to the table top. After this 24-hour period it can be attached to the table with double stick tape at the outer edges only. If a pencil line is drawn where the tape has been placed it will make an impression on the drafting vellum, so keep the tape at the outer edges of the surface.

The drafting machine (or parallel) is mounted right on top of this new surface. It is best cleaned with a household cleaner like Fantastik or Formula 409. Soap will clean it but drafting tape or dots will not adhere to it very well.

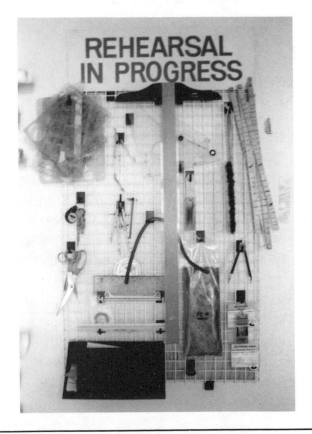

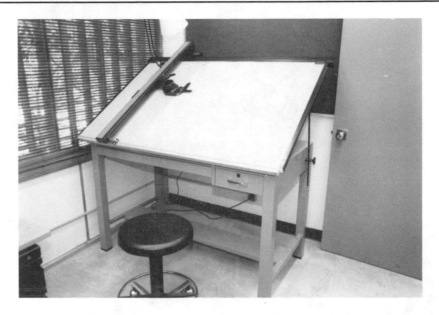

Paper and Machine

Vellum is the medium of choice for drafting. It is easy to draw on and erase, holds up fairly well to normal wear and tear, and is translucent enough to make blueprints from. It can be purchased in rolls of many different widths from which you cut your individual sheets for drafting. Vellum can also be bought on a pad of pre-cut sheets, and you can even buy individual pre-cut sheets. Buying it by the roll tends to be the most economical.

At the core of the draftsperson's equipment is the device which does most of the work when it comes to drawing perfect parallel horizontal and vertical lines. Some of these devices may draw perfectly parallel angled lines as well. These devices fall into one of three categories: the drafting machine, the parallel, and the T-square.

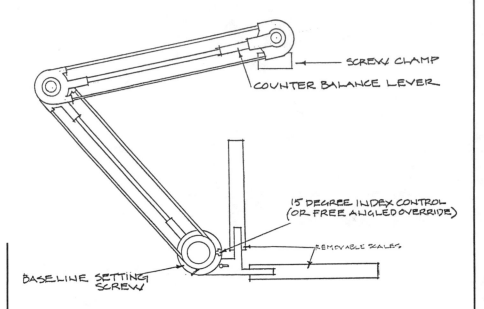

Drafting Machine

The drafting machine assists in drawing parallel horizontal and vertical lines by having two "arms" which are mounted permanently at 90° to each other. These removable "arms" have scales printed on them and can be interchanged with other scales. They come in a variety of lengths also ranging from 9 inches to about 2 feet in length.

The scale assembly rotates to aid in drawing any angle, theoretically eliminating the need for additional triangles to perform that function.

Cost: About $200.00

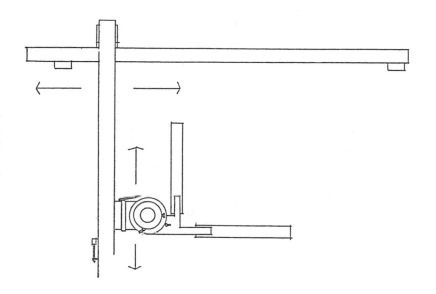

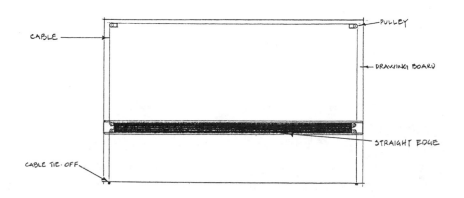

"V" (Vertical)-Track Drafting Machine

The V-track is a variation on the drafting machine. It is most handy on steeply inclined drafting tables. The scale assembly glides both horizontally and vertically along the machine. Like the regular drafting machine, its scale assembly also rotates for drafting angles. An advantage this variation has over the traditional drafting machine is the elimination of the need to lift the heavy assembly up off the paper each time you wish to move it. Moving the scale assembly around the drafting table is nearly effortless as it is supported by the vertical and horizontal support bars.

　Cost: About $300.00

Parallel Rule Straight Edge

The parallel rule straight edge is the simplest (and least expensive) of the mechanical drafting devices. It is simply a straight edge which glides up and down the table. It is kept very true by a cable which runs throughout it and is anchored to the table at four points. Variations in designs include ball bearing type rollers to help it glide over your drafting, clear drawing blades on each edge, and an under-the-board cable mounting capability.

　Sizes typically vary from 30 inches to 72 inches in 6 inch increments. Triangles and/or an adjustable triangle are needed to draw vertical lines and various angles.

　Cost:　36″ about $60.00
　　　　42″ about $67.00
　　　　54″ about $82.00

T-Square

The T-square is a low-tech non-mechanical drafting device. It is simply a straight edge that can be moved up and down the drafting table. The horizontal blade moves up and down the table while a vertical block holds it rigid (and therefore parallel) against the side of the drafting table. Uneven pressure can position the blade at an odd angle on the table. It must constantly be trued up with the non-drafting hand. It is usually made of maple with two Lucite edges. It is best to avoid painted T-squares as these often leave their paint behind on the vellum. They also come in stainless steel and aluminum.

Cost based on 36″ length: wood about $15.00
aluminum about $20.00
steel about $35.00

French Curve

Many variations of the French curve exist. A set of these curves allows the draftsperson to draw just about any complex curve.

Cost: About $5.00

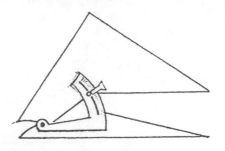

Adjustable Triangle

The adjustable triangle eliminates the need for an assortment of other triangles. It can be set at any angle. It is clear plastic and comes in several different sizes.

Cost: 8 inch base: about $10.00
10 inch base: about $12.00
12 inch base: about $15.00
larger sizes: $20.00 and up

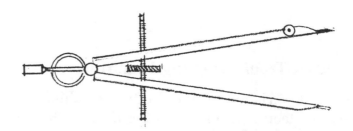

Bow Compass

The bow compass is used to draw circles. It has a sharp point at one end which sticks into the drafting surface and a lead holder at the other. It is adjustable so that circles of many different radii can be drawn. Compass variations include the beam compass which allows the draftsperson to draw unusually large circles.

Cost: About $15.00

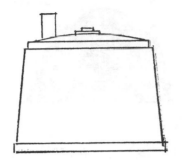

Lead Pointer

This device is used to sharpen the lead in a lead holder. Many variations are available including those that clamp onto the edge of the drafting table. They are not for sharpening a regular pencil.

Cost: $5.00 to $25.00

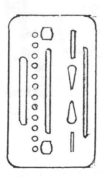

Eraser Shield

The eraser shield is a very thin piece of aluminum with many holes of various shapes. It is helpful in achieving pinpoint accuracy in your erasing. Many types and sizes are available.

Cost: About $.75

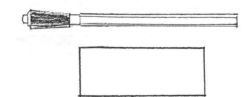

Eraser

A special white plastic eraser made just for drafting vellum is the best to use.

Cost: About $1.00

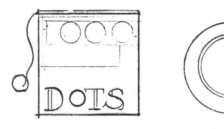

Drafting Dots (or Drafting Tape)

Drafting dots (and tape) hold your work to the table without tearing the corners of the paper when removed. The dots are an improvement over the tape in that there is no corner of a piece of tape to get stuck to the drafting machine.

Cost: About $2.00 to $5.00

Triangular Architect's Scale Rule

This tool usually contains 12 different measuring scales on 6 different sides—$\frac{3}{32}$, $\frac{3}{16}$, $\frac{1}{2}$, 1, $\frac{1}{8}$, $\frac{1}{4}$, $\frac{3}{8}$, $\frac{3}{4}$, $1\frac{1}{2}$, 3, and 16 (standard rule).

Cost: About $3.00

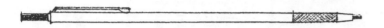

Lead Holder

The lead holder houses the drafting lead. There are 17 degrees of standard lead. Not all lead holders accept all 17. An alternative to using lead and a lead holder is a wooden drafting pencil which looks like a normal pencil except that it has no eraser. The lead holder lead must be sharpened in a special lead pointer but the wooden drafting pencil is sharpened in a pencil sharpener.

    Cost: About $4.00

    A package of a dozen leads will sell for about the same amount.

Stomp (Shading Tool)

This is a "stick" of compressed fiber that is used to blend graphite for the purpose of adding shade and texture to your drawings.

    Cost: About $2.00

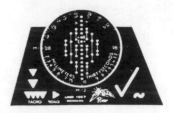

Lettering Guide

The lettering guide does not draw letters as its name implies but instead draws precise guidelines on which to make the letters. It is a must for drawing consistent guidelines quickly.

    Cost: $1.50

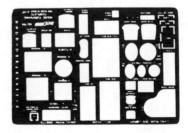

Furniture Template

The furniture template is used to draw plan views of furniture pieces in either ¼″ or ½″ scale. Many different rooms and styles are available. These templates are invaluable for allowing the proper amount of room in a floor plan for the intended furniture. They allow quick and accurate drawings of complicated furniture pieces.

    Cost: $4.00

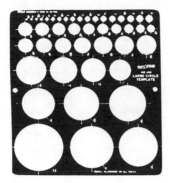

Circle Template

Particularly helpful in drawing smaller circles. When choosing a circle template be sure to get one that has lots of smaller circles that are difficult to draw with a compass. Large circles on these templates go unused for the most part as they can be drawn with a compass quite easily.

Cost: $3.00

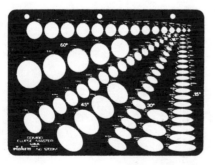

Ellipse Template

The ellipse template is an invaluable aid. There simply is no other way to do this otherwise very difficult job.

Cost: $5.00

Square Template

An excellent tool for drawing multiples of the same square over and over, such as the tops of newel posts in floor plans.

Cost: $4.00

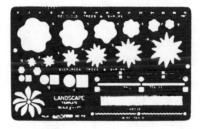

Landscape Template

Helpful for depicting foliage symbols in floor plans.

Cost: 4.00

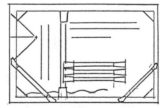

Muslin Flat Rear Elevation Template

A special template available by mail order only. (The Scenic Graphic Template from Lighting Associates, P.O. Box 299, Chester, CT 06412, 203-526-9315. Cost at time of publication was $5.50.). It is sometimes advertised in theater and lighting magazines.

Buying Drafting Supplies

A trip to a good drafting supply store will reveal many other templates that are available to make drafting scenery easier. You will even find many variations of the templates described above. Of course the prices will vary from store to store and city to city. If you find that the prices are significantly above these prices, try another store or brand of equipment. But don't buy too cheap. The best templates are made of a flexible plastic. Stay away from templates made of rigid plastic, like those found in drugstores and supermarkets.

The following list of equipment is an inventory of drafting tools that you will need right away. It is by no means a complete list of all of the drafting equipment available. Catalogs of drafting equipment fill up a book as thick as this one. It is instead intended as a starter kit upon which you can build over the years.

BASICS

T-square	$20.00*
adjustable triangle	20.00*
bow compass	15.00
eraser	1.00*
eraser shield	.75
drafting dots/tape	4.00*
architect's scale	3.00*
lettering guide	1.50*
furn. template ¼"	4.00
furn. template ½"	4.00
circle template	3.00
draft. vell. (24 × 36)	20.00
2H pencil	1.00*
household cleaner	2.00
sharpener	7.50*
total	$102.75

EXTRAS

drafting machine	200.00
v-track machine	300.00
parallel rule	60.00
drafting leads	2.00
lead holder	4.00
ellipse template	5.00
square template	4.00
landscape template	4.00
drafting powder	4.00
lead pointer	10.00
electric eraser	20.00
drafting brush	5.00
stomp	2.00

* These items are essential for the first few exercises in this workbook. The other BASIC items will not be needed quite so soon.

Getting Started at the Drafting Table

1. Before sitting down at the drafting table to work on your next project, get in the habit of thoroughly cleaning the surface of your table. A cleaner such as Fantastik® or Formula 409® is best, but soap and water can also be used. If you are using soap and water use more water than soap. It doesn't take too much to get the job done and the drafting dots will not stick to soap which has dried on the surface.

2. Next, clean all of your drafting equipment. This is important because graphite buildup on your tools will leave smudges and smears on the vellum.

3. Wash your hands before handling the vellum. It's surprising to discover the amount of graphite that very quickly builds up on your hands. You should check for graphite buildup on your hands and your tools often during each drafting session. Washing them periodically will keep your drafting free of smudges.

4. Align the blade of your parallel rule or drafting machine with the bottom of your table. Unlock it, align it so that it is parallel to the bottom, and then lock it up again. If you are using a drafting machine you will also need to align the scales to make certain that they are at 90° to each other; use a large triangle to help you.

5. If you are using a drafting machine, place the scale assembly near the bottom edge of the table top. Position the horizontal scale at least an inch away from the bottom edge of the table. Place the bottom edge of your sheet of vellum right along the top edge of the horizontal scale. The next step is to place the paper carefully on the drafting table.

Tape down the four corners. Be sure to leave room on the right or left edge of your table for drafting equipment if you are not using a side table for tool storage.

If you are using a T-square or parallel rule, place it at least an inch away from the bottom edge of the table top. Align the bottom edge of your sheet of vellum along the top edge of your T-square or parallel. (An alternative is to place the paper along the top edge of the raised center finger grip on the T-square or parallel.) Next tape down the top corners of the vellum. Then place the blade (by slightly lifting it off of the paper) at the top of the sheet and slowly glide it down toward the bottom stopping just before reaching the bottom edge. This smooths out the paper, and removes air which might otherwise be trapped underneath. The resulting vacuum helps the paper adhere to the drafting surface. Now, tape the bottom two corners of the paper.

6. Draw a border around your sheet using either one medium weight (USITT = "thick") line, or two heavyweight (USITT = "extra thick") lines about ¾″ away from the edge of the vellum. More about this later.

7. Very lightly outline the eventual position of your title block. Drawing your title block as the first step on a new sheet of drafting is not a good idea. You may end up throwing the sheet out due to some catastrophic drawing error and will have wasted a lot of time drawing the title block. It is a good idea, however, to reserve the space for the block by lightly outlining its position.

2. Lettering

Not all of the information about the scenery you draft will be communicated purely through lines. A great deal of the data will be conveyed through printed words and numbers. The words will take the form of labels and notes which identify views or describe materials and techniques. The numbers will be the dimensions that graphically reveal the size and placement of scenic elements. All of these notes and dimensions that you put on your drawings must be as clear and exact as any precision drafted line.

Some people seem to have an affinity for neat printing, while others simply gave up somewhere around the fourth grade. For those of us in this latter category it means that we will have to learn all over again how to form each letter and number so that our notes, labels, and dimensions are distinct, legible, and unmistakable. Many a 6 foot wall was constructed at 8 feet because of a poorly scrawled out number.

What follows next are a couple of observations about why some lettering styles are easier to read than others and a style sheet explaining letter formation. None of this is presented as an attempt to teach you any particular style of lettering. Indeed, the rather uninteresting and stilted letters that are introduced here are not meant to be an example of the ideal draftsperson's lettering. They are offered only as a way of laying out some basic rules to help you achieve neatness and legibility. As you copy the styles in the style sheet and practice each letter slowly, over and over, you will begin forming letters that are legible.

When you reach the stage of being confident with your lettering, and as you undertake your first drafting projects, your lettering will look quite close to these uninteresting and stilted letters. This is both good and bad! Good in the sense that your letters will at least be readable, and that's half the battle. But bad in the sense that your letters will be quite artificial, rigid, uninteresting, and lacking style (not to mention that it will take a painfully long time to form each of these perfect letters). However, as your lettering becomes more second nature, and as your speed picks up, a transformation will take place. Your letters will still be clear and understandable but you will begin developing a *style*. Your letters and numbers will begin to achieve a tone that is uniquely yours, highly readable, and quick to draw.

This will not happen for quite a while, and unless you do a lot of drafting it can take a year or so. But there is a way to speed up the process. If lots of practice is the key to success, then why not practice all the time? Whenever you write out a shopping list or take a phone message, rather than falling back on your old chicken scratching, practice your best draftsperson's printing. Every chance you get, use all "caps" and Gothic letters, based on the square, to do such things as take class notes, write a letter, or write down a phone number. If you stick to this regimen faithfully your letters will have a professional style and clarity in a relatively short amount of time. Many draftspersons with poor penmanship letter quite well (myself included), so don't say that you can't do it!

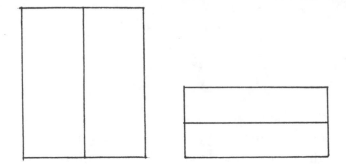

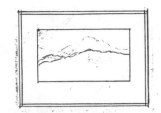

Stability

A good readable letter must look stable. That is, it can't look like it could fall over in a breeze created by opening the scene shop door. To make some letters look stable you must be aware of, and counteract the effects of, a common optical illusion. This optical illusion is demonstrated above. The line drawn across the middle of the rectangle can appear to actually be drawn just below the center. If the top rectangle looks bigger due to this phenomenon then it will look more massive, heavier. The whole object will appear unstable—ready to fall over.

This can be a problem with the letters B, E, K, S, X, Z, and the numbers 3 and 8. If the middle bar of the letter or intersection of lines does not appear to be at or above the halfway point in the letter's height, then the letter will be unstable, poorly formed.

Picture framers have a similar problem with the mat that borders the picture. If the bottom side of the mat is cut to the same width as the other three sides it will actually appear smaller due to the visual weight of the picture bearing down on it. To solve this problem the bottom side of the mat is almost always cut slightly wider.

You can get around this stability problem with letters and numbers by placing the middle bar, or intersection

lines of letters, slightly above the center. The trick to this precision placement is the use of guidelines. *No letter or number should ever be formed without first drawing guidelines.* Each line of letters or numbers will have a set of three guidelines. You can even make things easier by placing the center guideline slightly above center.

Proportions

Letters on a sheet of drafting are always capitalized. All the lettering that you do from now on should be done with simple, single-stroke capital letters. These letters should be based on a square. As you will see, some will be wider and some will be narrower, but the square shape is a good guide to their formation.

It is much easier to read a

LOW WIDE LETTER

than a

HIGH NARROW ONE

As you form each of your letters, note that vertical strokes in single stroke Gothic letters are always made downward. Horizontal strokes are always drawn from left to right (right to left if you are lefthanded).

Letter Groups Style Sheet

Here is a style sheet for drafting letters and numbers. It is divided into family groups. Each family member is related to the other by the way it looks and/or by certain rules about letter formation. Remember, mastering these letters is only a starting point in developing your own personal lettering style.

The first three steps in conquering this style sheet are practice, practice, and practice. You should drill yourself on each letter over and over in ¼″ high letters. Almost all the letters that you draw while actually drafting will be about half this size, but if you can conquer them in this scale then the smaller versions will be a snap. This is like the French soccer hero who shared his formula for success in manipulating a soccer ball. He revealed that his secret was hours and hours of practice with a tennis ball when he was young. The tennis ball is much smaller and extremely difficult to maneuver with your feet. But after mastering the sport of tennis ball soccer he became a legend not long after it came time to move up to the larger and "simpler" soccer ball.

Practice your lettering by laying down a sheet of vellum. Use your lettering guide (instructions for its use are included with your lettering guide) to fill up a sheet or two with nothing but sets of very light weight. Each set should have three lines and be about a ¼″ apart. Practice each letter group until you are able to draw the letters perfectly (and not just by accident). Then move on to the next group.

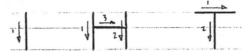

I, H, and T comprise the first family group. They are the simplest to form. Perfecting these letters will help you out with all the others. If you find that making the seemingly simple vertical strokes is the most upsetting thing that you have ever done in your life, stop and catch your breath. You may want to throw in some random *vertical* guidelines as well. Use your lettering guide for this by laying the bottom of the guide on your horizontal arm while drawing short vertical strokes every inch or so with the vertical side of the guide. All letters relate to the perfect square. In this group the H and T would make a square if the tops and bottoms or sides were continued. The stem of the T is centered on the letter.

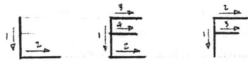

L, E, and F comprise the next group. Notice the lengths of the number 2, 3, and 4 strokes on the E. Like the E, many letters should be made narrower at the top in order to reduce the visual weight of the top half. The result is a more stable looking letter. In each letter above, the number 1 and 2 strokes are exactly the same length. They form two sides of the square.

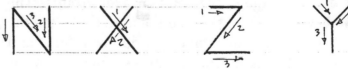

Note that in this group the tops of the X and Z are narrower than the bottoms. Again, this helps with their stability. The width of each letter at the base is equal to the height. The width of the top of the Y is equal to its height.

The V, A, K group finds us wrestling a bit with these rules of stability. The bridge of the A is not at or above the center guideline but is instead ⅓ of the way up from the base. The same is true of the end of the second stroke of the K. If the third stroke of the K were to continue up, it would meet the top of the first stroke. The bases of the A and the K and the width of the V are equal to their heights.

M and W are the widest letters. Each one goes a bit outside of the imaginary square. Be careful about making the width of the letter points no wider than each of the strokes that form them.

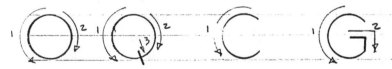

Now that you have vanquished the straight-stroke letters, it's time to meet the curved and circular groups. The O, Q, C, and G group might take a little more time than the last group. If you don't cheat, and you do form the O and Q in two strokes, then make the left stroke longer (it seems to be easier that way). The tail of the Q is not to be drawn curved. It is a short, straight stroke. Note that the bar of the G is half way between the top and bottom guidelines. Each letter fits perfectly inside the imaginary square.

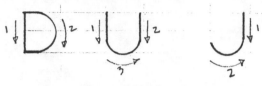

Observe that the top and bottom of the curved strokes of the D are horizontal. Each of these letters is a bit narrower than the width of the square.

In this group it is important to note that the beginnings of the 2, 3, and 4 strokes of each of these letters is a straight line. The width of each of these letters at their widest points is equal to their heights. The top of the B is slightly narrower than the bottom (rule of stability). Fewer strokes are needed for the smaller versions of these letters.

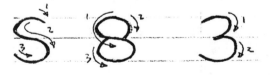

With the S, 8, and 3 group you want to avoid the flat tops of the previous group; especially in the 3. It can be confused with a 5 if it has a flat top.

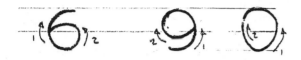

The "lobes" of the 6 and the 9 are ⅔ of the way up or down the letter. The number 0 is narrower than the letter O.

The curve of the 2 reverses at the center guideline. The second stroke of the 7 ends directly below the center of the top stroke.

Like the letter A, the number 4 seems to be an exception to the rule of stability. The third stroke is ⅓ of the way up from the bottom of the letter.

Some Rules for Lettering

1. With few exceptions, all lettering on a sheet of drafting should be about ⅛" high. It actually will look better slightly shorter than this by about 1/16".

Exceptions include:

a. the title of a view (<u>ELEVATION</u>, <u>SECTION</u>, <u>PLAN</u>, etc.)

b. a title of a sheet (<u>LAUREY'S FARMHOUSE REAR ELEVATIONS</u>, etc.) at the bottom center of the sheet or in the title block

c. the title of the show (<u>OKLAHOMA!</u>, etc.) in the title block

2. View titles, sheet titles, and the title of the show in the title block should be in letters that are about ¼" high.

3. Guidelines must be drawn for all letters.

4. Guidelines must be drawn for all dimensions and other numbers.

5. Lettering choices (style, heights, widths, etc.) must stay consistent throughout the entire set of working drawings.

Project 1   Lettering

1. Draw a border around your sheet ¾″ away from each edge. Borders should always be drawn as one heavy-weight (USITT = "extra thick") line or two medium-weight (USITT = "thick") lines drawn a line width away from each other.

2. Fill the sheet with ¼″ sets of very light-weight guidelines. Leave about a ¼″ between the sets.

3. Practice drawing ¼″ letters in family groups in the following manner:

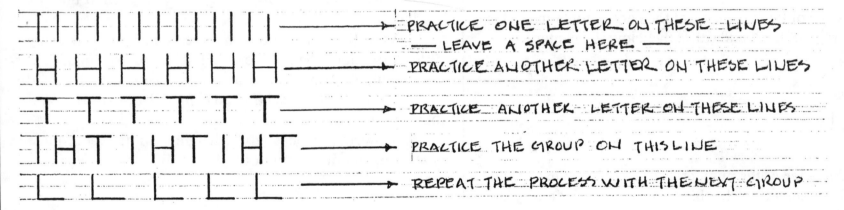

PRACTICE ONE LETTER ON THESE LINES
— LEAVE A SPACE HERE —
PRACTICE ANOTHER LETTER ON THESE LINES
PRACTICE ANOTHER LETTER ON THESE LINES
PRACTICE THE GROUP ON THIS LINE
REPEAT THE PROCESS WITH THE NEXT GROUP

4. After mastering the letters at ¼″, repeat step 3 using ⅛″ letters. This will take more than one sheet.

3. Title Blocks

The title block is the name given to the approximately 3″ × 5″ information filled rectangle found in the lower right-hand corner of every sheet of drafting. It is a concise detailed directory concerning the drafting found on that sheet. Its most important function is to identify the name of the show. But it also discloses important details regarding which scale to use when making measurements, where the set is being used, and when the construction must be complete. The title block is placed about an inch away from the bottom right-hand borders.

The title block must include the following elements:

a. NAME OF THE SHOW—Since this is a title it should be written in ¼″ high letters. Even larger letters are used for the show title sometimes. Some draftspersons and designers prefer to use rub-on letters or a lettering template (different from a lettering guide) for the title. It results in a very distinctive look but can be quite time consuming if there are many sheets of drafting. The show name will be the only item in the title block which uses this letter size. As a title it must also be underlined. Everything else will be in ⅛″ letters except for the sheet number.

b. DIRECTOR'S NAME—As a courtesy, this name heads the list of names in the title block. The format is usually something like "DIRECTED BY: (name)"

c. DESIGNER'S NAME—The second name listed in the title block. Its format should be identical to the director's.

d. DRAFTSPERSON'S NAME (optional)—This name should be included only if it is different from the designer's.

Again, the same format is used. Frequently however, the draftsperson's name is indicated by initials only.

e. PRODUCTION SITE—This is the theater, studio, or sound stage where the event is taking place.

f. PERTINENT DATES—The date that the drawing is completed is often the only date needed on the sheet. Sometimes it is necessary to include other dates such as the date construction is to be completed, the date that the set is to be loaded into the space, or the date that the taping or filming begins. This extra information is helpful to the shop responsible for building the set for purposes of scheduling and pacing their efforts.

g. APPROVAL SPACE—This is a space allocated for the initials of such persons as the director, producer, etc. Getting these initials at the beginning can be quite helpful to you later on in the production process.

h. SCALE—The scale is written as ½″ = 1′-0″. Sometimes you will find yourself drafting a full scale detail drawing, in which case you would simply put FULL SCALE. If the majority of the drawings on the sheet are all at different scales then you should indicate the scale of each drawing under the drawing title and in the title block write "VARIES."

i. SHEET NUMBER—This should be in the lower right-hand corner of the title block for the convenience of anyone who might be flipping through the plans looking for a particular sheet. It should be a large (at least 1″ high) number. Here too rub-on letters or a lettering template are often used. Above the number it should read "SHEET #." Below the number should be printed "OF (the number of sheets in the plans)."

j. TITLE OF SHEET—A sheet title is sometimes placed underneath the show title. For instance after the show title OKLAHOMA! you might place a sheet title such as PLAN —LAUREY'S FARMHOUSE.

k. STAMP SPACE—This space is for a stamp such as a union or professional affiliation stamp.

The title block is usually hand drawn (medium-weight line) on each sheet of drafting as a last step to completing that sheet. But there are other options available which are designed to speed up or semi-automate this process. Many designers have their vellum pre-printed with the title block already on it. The designer's name, address, telephone number, and even a logo become a permanent part of every sheet. "SHEET #" and "OF (number of sheets)" are also pre-printed. Blank spaces are left where specific data relating to each show is then inscribed. These spaces would incorporate the name of the show, the director, the sheet number, important dates, space for approval, the scale of the drawing, and other optional elements of information.

Another method of semi-automating the title block process is with a pre-printed self-adhesive transfer. These can be made up at most printing establishments and are fairly inexpensive. They are pre-printed with the same sorts of information found on a pre-printed sheet of vellum. After a paper backing is peeled off, the title block is applied to the drafting vellum. The specific show information can then be filled in. It is very difficult if not impossible to tell a pre-printed adhesive from a pre-printed sheet of drafting once it has been blueprinted or photocopied.

Some designers and art directors use a large rubber stamp with the same pre-printed information described above. The block is stamped onto the vellum and then that particular production's information is filled in by hand. All three methods are excellent approaches to saving lots of expensive drafting time.

Here are some examples of various title blocks. A good title block does not call too much attention to itself. When designing your own distinctive title block you will undoubtedly want to design something intricate and fancy. It is important to remember that the more complex it is, the more time it will take to draw it. You will come to loathe any over-designed title block after drawing it for the tenth time. When designing your block, keep in mind the time it will take to draw it.

NIGHT OF THE
IGUANA 4 OF 7

S.D.- 355
SCENIC DESIGNER

SIGNATURE RICH ROSE

DIR: MICHAEL GORDON
DES: RICH ROSE
LITTLE THEATER
5·24·91
SCALE: 1/2" = 1'-0"

UCLA THEATER ARTS DEPARTMENT
APPROVED FOR PRODUCTION
DIRECTOR:
TECHNICAL DIRECTOR:
DESIGN SUPERVISOR: RICH ROSE

	SHEET 1 OF	PRODUCER STANLEY DONEN
ABC TELEVISION NETWORK HOLLYWOOD Production Services Department		DIRECTOR MARTY PASETTA
		ART DIR. ROY CHRISTOPHER
SHOW 58TH ANNUAL ACADEMY AWARDS NO.	APPROVED	DRAFTSMAN GSR
		LIGHTING DIR.
SET TITLE "HOLLYWOOD PROFILE"		TECHNICAL DIR.
SHOW DATE 3·24· VTR DATE 3·24· DATE DRAWN 2·13·		SCALE 1/2"=1'-0"

GREASE

SCALE: 1/4"=1'-0'	APPROVED BY	DRAWN BY GSR
DATE: 5·1·		
CL · SECTION - LA MIRADA CIVIC		
DESIGNER GREGORY S. RICHMAN		DRAWING NUMBER 2 OF 9

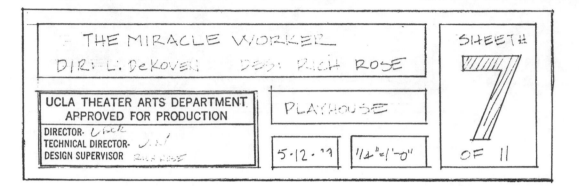

THE MIRACLE WORKER
DIR: L. DeKOVEN   DES: RICH ROSE

SHEET # 7

OF 11

UCLA THEATER ARTS DEPARTMENT
APPROVED FOR PRODUCTION
DIRECTOR-
TECHNICAL DIRECTOR-
DESIGN SUPERVISOR

PLAYHOUSE

5·12·99   1/4"=1'-0"

B R U C E   R Y A N

production design • art direction

1040 Monterey Road • South Pasadena • California • 91030 • (818) ...

Scale	Drawing Title	Drawing No.
1/2 = 1'-0"	DOWN STAGE RIGHT UNIT	
Drawn By	Production	
T. SHIMOJIMA	M.T.V. MUSIC AWARDS	
Date Drawn	Set Up Date	Show Date
JULY 6, '99		

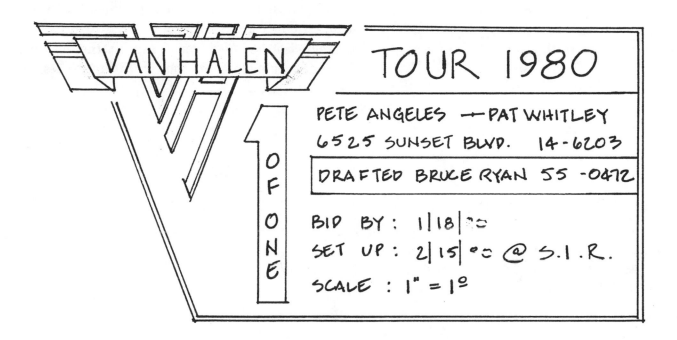

Checklist

Use this checklist to be sure that you are including the necessary information in your title blocks.

- ☐ Show title
- ☐ Name of director
- ☐ Name of scenic designer/art director
- ☐ Event site
- ☐ Drawing date(s)
- ☐ Approval space

- ☐ Scale
- ☐ Sheet number information

Optional Information:
- ☐ Name (or initials) of draftsperson
- ☐ Title of sheet
- ☐ Space for stamps of any professional affiliations

Project 2   Title Blocks

1. Draw a ¾″ border around a sheet of vellum.

2. Design 3 title blocks and draft them onto your sheet. Leave the lower right-hand corner of the paper free of any drawing.

3. Choose the block design you like the best and place it in the lower right-hand corner—1″ away from the bottom and side border. Feel free to modify the design you choose to incorporate elements that will improve its design.

4. Line Weights

Line "weight" actually refers to the *thickness* of a drafted line. In drafting, different line thicknesses have very different meanings. They are a language in themselves and can give a meaning other than intended if used improperly. Scenic drafting uses four different line weights. Layout weight lines (sometimes referred to as phantom lines or ghost lines) are the thinnest. Next come light-weight lines (also known as thin), medium-weight lines (also known as thick), and finally, heavy-weight lines (also known as extra thick lines and sometimes called section lines). The terms thin, thick, and extra thick are the terms that the USITT (United States Institute for Theater Technology), in a move toward standardization of scenic drafting, has chosen to label these line weights. This book will use the USITT terms and the more common terms for these weights interchangeably.

No matter what you call them, it's important that all of your lines show up crisp, solid, and with the right amount of darkness and contrast on the paper. If they are too light they will blueprint or photocopy poorly.

Achieving Distinct Line Weights

To achieve these different weights or thicknesses any one of four different methods may be used:

1. Draw lines next to each other, with a slight overlap, to achieve thicker lines.

2. Press harder on the pencil for a thicker line.

3. Use a different lead weight (four different lead holders or pencils) for each line weight.

4. Any combination of the above.

Lead Weight Scale

There are many different lead weights (degrees of hardness or softness of the lead) available for drawing. You can buy pencils or leads in sets or individually. Here is a list of the most common lead weights from softest to hardest:

8B, 7B, 6B, 5B, 4B, 3B—These very soft leads will result in an extremely thick line and deep black color. They need sharpening quite often and are normally used for sketching and drawing.

2B, B, HB—These soft leads will result in a thick line and black color. These weights need sharpening often and are good for thicker lines in drafting scenery.

F, H—These medium leads will result in a medium to thick line and dark gray color. These are excellent weights for lettering unless you have a heavy drafting hand.

2H, 3H, 4H, 5H, 6H—These hard leads will result in medium to thin lines and a typical gray lead color. These are the weights to use for medium to thin lines in drafting.

7H, 8H, 9H, 10H—These very hard leads will result in very light, thin lines. They are not recommended for drafting scenery.

Some pencils have number designations alone without a letter following. Here is a list of those, cross referenced with their drafting pencil equivalents:

#1 = 3B

#2 = B

#2½ = HB

#3 = F

#4 = 2H

#5 = 4H

If you will be using one pencil to achieve different line thicknesses, you should start out by using a 2H pencil. Some people are more heavy or light handed than others and you may find that you fall into one category or the other. You may find that a 2H pencil is too soft or too hard, in which case you should switch to a harder pencil (3H) or a softer pencil (H). But for now give 2H a try.

If you will be using four different pencils to achieve different line thickness, you should start out with:

a 4H pencil for layout lines

a 3H pencil for light-weight lines

a 2H pencil for medium-weight lines

an H pencil for heavy-weight lines.

Again, you may find that you are heavy or light handed and may need to slide up or down the scale. If you are heavy handed you will want to go with a harder pencil in each case, and if you are light-handed you may want to go with softer pencils.

The difference between the four line weights is subtle. It is important that you achieve a strong, disciplined uniformity in producing them. You need to accomplish a uniformity within each line. That is, a consistent line that doesn't go from thick to thin and then back to thick again all in one line. You also need to achieve a uniformity between lines. A medium-weight line on one drawing must be the same as a medium-weight line on another drawing. Poor line uniformity could have disastrous results in the scene shop. What a carpenter thought was the edge of a scenic unit might have actually been a dimension line. The result being a scenic unit which is now three feet too big.

Obtaining Consistent Lines

1. Sharpen your pencil frequently while drafting. At first this seems tedious and time consuming, but it is absolutely necessary to obtain crisp, focused, uniform lines. It will soon become a routine habit.

2. PULL the pencil and never push it while drawing a line.

3. Rotate, or rock, the pencil slowly back and forth in your fingers as you draw each line. This prevents a flat edge from forming and keeps the end of the lead pointed. It will be tricky and awkward at first but it will become quite natural after a little practice.

4. Never draw on a bare, too hard, or too soft drawing surface. Your lines will blur and they will never blueprint or photocopy clearly. Your drawing table should be covered with a professional drafting table surface available at any good drafting supply store. It comes in rolls and several colors. You could cut it somewhat larger than your drafting table and let it lie flat for 24 hours before attaching it to the surface with double-faced tape. Place the tape at the outer edges only and not in the area where you will be drafting. Next, trim it to exact size.

5. Never draw a line freehand. The pencil lead should always be in contact with, and guided by, a straight edge. This could be your drafting machine, parallel, T-square, or a triangle that is touching one of those.

6. After completely laying out a sheet of drafting with all of your views in layout line, go over it (in the approximate weight) with your drafting machine from top to bot-

tom drawing all of your horizontal lines. Start at the top and work your way to the bottom. Then draw all of your vertical lincs. Start on the left and work your way to the right. Then draw all of your angled lines. This technique keeps the passes of the tools over the drawing to a minimum and reduces the chance of smudges and smearing.

Accomplishing a superior and consistent caliber in your lines will not come right away and it is not easy. Like lettering, it is something that you will always be working at and will come only through lots of practice.

Layout Weight Line

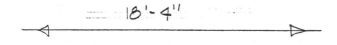

This is the lightest or thinnest of the four line weights used in scenic drafting. It will not show up in the blueprint or photocopy most of the time, and it shouldn't.

Its uses are:
1. Guidelines for letting and dimensions.
2. Laying out your drawings on a sheet of drafting.

Light-Weight (Thin) Line   .3mm

This line is intended to be quite thin yet it should show up quite nicely on the blueprint.

Its uses are:
1. Dimension lines.
2. Extension lines.
3. Leader lines.

4. Dashed lines representing hidden construction elements.

5. Dashed lines representing alternate positions of scenery.

6. Special dashed center line.

7. Break lines.

8. Dashed plaster, ceiling, set, or proscenium lines.

Medium-Weight (Thick) Line   .5mm

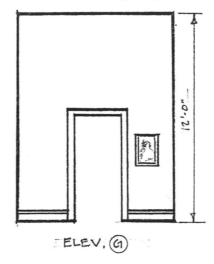

Most of your drafting will be done with the medium-weight line. It represents the visible outline of any object being drafted. All other line weights are based on the medium-weight line. They are either thicker or thinner. For this reason it is important that you master the medium-weight line to draw the outlines of the objects; the outline of the flat, the outline of the moldings, and the outline of the picture hung on the wall. Light-weight lines are used for dimension and extension lines.

Its uses are:
1. Drawing the visible outline of an object.

2. Drawing the visible outline of all detail applied to that object (painted or three dimensional).

3. The weight used for all letters and numbers.

4. Drawing the theater architecture.

5. A drafting sheet double-line border.

6. The title block lines.

7. Filling in the space inside the heavy outline of a section view of a solid object.

Heavy-Weight (Extra Thick) Line   .9mm

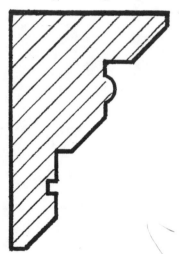

Sometimes referred to as a section line, the heavy-weight line is the thickest of the four line weights. If you are using one pencil to draw all of your line weights you will need to draw at least two or three medium-weight lines next to each other to obtain a heavy-weight line.

Its uses are:

1. Drawing the outline in a <u>SECTION</u> or cut-through view of a solid object.

2. Drawing walls, drapes, cycs, and other tall set pieces in a <u>PLAN</u>.

3. Drawing <u>REVOLVED PLAN</u> views.

4. Drawing <u>REVOLVED SECTION</u> views.

5. A drafting sheet single line border.

6. Dashed cutting plane line.

Project 3   Line Weights

1. Draw a ¾″ border around your sheet.

2. In layout weight line, outline the eventual position of your title block in the lower right hand corner. Remember to place the title block about 1″ away from the bottom and side borders.

3. Complete this line weight project by following the directions in steps 4–11 below. All lines in this project should:

—start 3″ from the left border

—be drawn 12″ long

—be placed ¼″ apart

The first line should be 2″ from the top border.

4. Draw 5 layout weight lines ¼″ apart, horizontally.

5. Draw 5 light-weight lines ¼″ apart, horizontally.

6. Draw 5 medium-weight lines ¼″ apart, horizontally.

7. Draw 5 heavy-weight lines ¼″ apart, horizontally.

8. Draw one layout-weight line followed by one light-weight line, followed by one heavy-weight line (all ¼″ apart).

9. Fill the page with these alternating line weights until you are 1″ away from the bottom border.

10. Keep all of your lines at least 1″ away from your title block.

11. Complete your title block.

SOLID LINES

Type		Weight
DIMENSION	⊢— 4'-4" —⊣	LIGHT (THIN)
VISIBLE OUTLINE		MEDIUM (THICK)
SECTION OUTLINE		HEAVY (EXTRA THICK)
SHEET BORDER		1 HEAVY OR 2 MEDIUM LINES
LEADER LINE		LIGHT
SECTION INTERIOR		LIGHT, EVENLY SPACED AT 45° ANGLE

DASHED LINES

Type		Weight
CUTTING PLANE	A — — — A'	HEAVY
HIDDEN CONSTRUCTION		LIGHT
PLASTER, CEILING SET, PROSCENIUM		LIGHT
CENTER LINE		LIGHT
BREAK		LIGHT
PHANTOM (ALTERNATE POSITION)		LIGHT

LINE WEIGHT USAGE CHART

(BASED ON USITT GRAPHICS)

5. Dimensions

All scenery is drafted "in scale." To scale a drawing means to choose a specified increment to represent a measured foot. The specified increment in scenic drafting is usually ½". The ½" scale (½" = 1"-0") is small enough to allow placement of many scenic units on a manageable size sheet of paper, yet is large enough to be able to specify most detail. For <u>DETAIL</u> drawings the scale is often larger; 1" or 3" for example, or even as big as FULL SCALE (1" = 1") for smaller subjects. Floor <u>PLANS</u> and <u>CENTER LINE VERTICAL SECTIONS</u> are often drawn at a smaller scale: ¼" = 1'-0". This is due to the fact that the size of the architecture of the performance space sometimes requires an awkwardly large sheet of paper to get it all in if it were drawn in ½" scale.

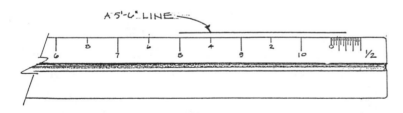

Scale Rule

To begin drafting in scale you must first learn to read the scale rule. The example above shows a scale rule ready to draw a line in ½" scale. (Please note that not all scale rules follow the same design as the one illustrated here.) Here are the steps involved in making a 5'-0" long line:

1. You can't measure air! To draw a specific line you must always have a preliminary line drawn on your paper. In layout weight line, draw a line that you estimate to be longer than the line you intend to draw.

2. Turn your scale so that it is below (for horizontal lines) or to the right (for vertical lines) of the layout line you just drew. This is so that the numbers on the scale are right side up. Put the scale right side up next to the line.

3. Place the zero mark of the scale where the line is to begin.

NOTE: If you wanted to draw a 5'-6" long line, you would place the 6" mark (which can be found to the right of the zero) at the beginning of your line rather than the zero. You would then follow the same steps below for the 5' long line (see example).

4. Place a mark at the precise beginning of your line by positioning the just-sharpened point of your pencil on the paper and twirling it back and forth a few times. This makes a tiny mark that will disappear when the line is drawn.

5. Now do the same thing where the other end of the line is to be. In this particular case you do not see a 5' mark on the scale. In fact you only see the foot-specifying designations of the even numbered feet. That is because this edge of the scale contains two different scales. For the 5' mark you would use the 8 which is located between the 4 and the 6. Because of this scale-sharing situation you need to stay on your toes. Notice that the designers of the scale have helped you out some by putting all of the ½"

scale numbers higher than the 1″ scale numbers but it is still quite easy to get confused.

6. Remove your scale, line up your drafting machine with the marks, and draw your line. Never use your scale rule as a straight edge to draw with. Always draw a line with a straight edge. You should only draw with your drafting machine or a triangle that is touching your drafting machine.

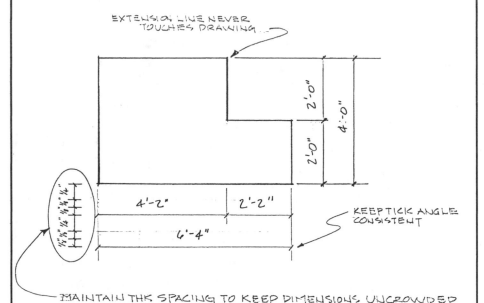

Here is an object that is properly dimensioned. Notice that in each case every dimension is made up of five parts:

1. GUIDELINES—Every number and letter require three guidelines. Dimensions are always a maximum of ⅛″ tall and can be a little smaller.

2. DIMENSION NUMBERS—There happen to be two accepted systems of displaying feet and inches when dimensioning scenery.

THEATRICAL—This first system is the most traditional of the two. The numbers must always be written as feet and inches with a hyphen in between. A five foot dimension is written as 5′-0″. It is never written as 5′. 12″ is always written as 1′-0″. Dimensions smaller than 12″ are written as inches only. 11″ is 11″ and not 0′-11″. That could be mistaken as 6′-11″.

FILM/TELEVISION—This second system is used widely in the realm of film and television. Feet and inch marks are not used at all. Instead the inches are placed above a dash that is placed to the right of the feet. $5\frac{6}{\text{—}}$ means 5′-6″, $5\frac{0}{\text{—}}$ means 5′-0″, and $0\frac{6}{\text{—}}$ means 6″, but so does 6″. Because this system is so quick, it is extremely popular in the "supersonic" world of television and film drafting.

No matter which system you use, there are still some factors common to both. In order to keep the drawing uncrowded, the top of any dimension number must never be any closer than ¼″ away from the scenery being drafted or from another dimension line. Vertical dimension numbers should never be written horizontally but rather are written vertically as if to be read from the right edge of the paper. They should never be written upside down or as if to be read from the left side of the sheet either. Dimension numbers should always be in or above the dimension line and never below.

3. DIMENSION LINE—(Also called a witness line) This is a single, light-weight line that either has the dimension above it or is broken with the dimension centered inside of it. The dimension line closest to the drawing should be no closer than ½″ in order to prevent confusing it with the edge of the object.

4. DIMENSION ARROW—The arrow is full and open (not filled in solid). The arrow tips must touch the exten-

sion lines. "Ticks" are being used more and more instead of arrows.

5. EXTENSION LINE—The extension line is also a light-weight line. It never touches the object but instead starts at about ⅛″ away from the object being dimensioned.

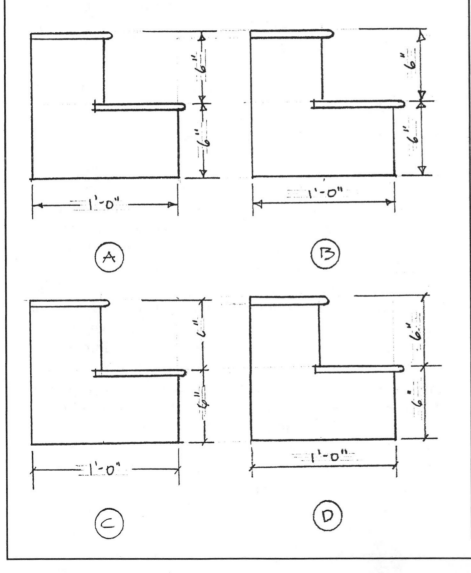

Dimensioning Systems

The previous illustration represents four accepted systems for proper dimensioning. While any one of them is correct, it is important that you stay with one system for any given set of plans. Mixing systems can lead to errors in interpreting your dimensions.

SYSTEM A breaks the dimension line and inserts the dimension inside of it. It uses open arrows. This is the most traditional dimensioning system.

SYSTEM B doesn't break the dimension line. The dimension is placed above the dimension line. It too uses open arrows. It is quicker to draw than system A.

SYSTEM C like system A breaks the dimension line and inserts the dimension inside of it. Instead of arrows it uses ticks. Ticks are quicker to draw and are used quite frequently in television and film drafting where speed is extremely important. A tick should always be at about 45°, stay consistent in terms of direction, and never be more than ⅛″ long.

SYSTEM D doesn't break the dimension line and uses ticks rather than arrows. It is the quickest of the four systems. For extra emphasis when using ticks rather than arrows, it is acceptable to have the dimension line extend about ⅛″ beyond the extension line.

Dimension Arrows

Dimension arrows must be full and open. Closed arrows and half arrows are reserved for leader lines (discussed in the section on ELEVATIONS). The arrow must be thin and have a long tip. The tip of the arrow should be a single, thin, light-weight line.

The three strokes which make up the end of the arrow

should be combined into one single line width. Notice the order of the strokes that make up an arrow in the illustration below.

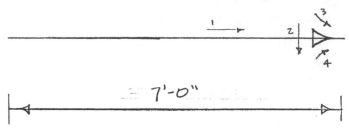

STROKE 1 of the arrow (including the tip) is the dimension line itself.

STROKE 2 places the base of the arrow. Keep this short. Your goal is a very thin arrow. Thick arrows will waste valuable drafting space on the page.

STROKE 3 places the top half of the arrow. It is a curved line that starts at the top of the arrow base and meets the dimension line at the midpoint between the base and the tip. Never draw this stroke to the tip.

STROKE 4 is the bottom half of the arrow and the final step. It should be a perfect mirror image of the top half.

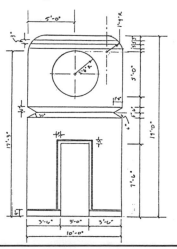

The previous piece of scenery has most of the dimensioning examples that you are likely to encounter. Notice that in this example similar dimensioning problems are being solved in several different ways. There is usually never one definitive way to solve a dimensioning issue.

It is critical that you don't under-dimension your scenery. No dimension should be left for anyone to sit and figure out. This wastes expensive shop time and opens the door for others, less skilled than you in drafting, to make errors. To get a sense of how much dimensioning you need, put yourself in the place of the carpenter who must build the scenery.

The Three Dimensioning Tiers

There is a hierarchy of at least three dimensioning levels that are needed on a drawing; detail *size*, detail *placement*, and overall *size*. You must complete each step before going on to the next, and you must complete all three before you can consider your dimensioning complete. This is how you should go about planning your dimensions.

1. Dimension the SIZE of all details that are *on* the scenery that you are drafting (but not the overall sizes of the scenic element itself). These might be sizes of openings for doors and windows, widths and lengths of moldings, etc.

2. When that is complete, pore over the object again and dimension the PLACEMENT of each of these details. For instance you would indicate the distance of a window opening to the edge of the flat. Next it might be the distance of a window bottom from the bottom of the flat. The sole purpose of this wave of dimensioning is to position the objects on the scenery for the carpenter.

As a rule of thumb, any part of the scenery that does not touch a physical edge of the unit must be "nailed down" with both a vertical and a horizontal dimension. This includes the center of every circle or arc.

3. The final level of dimensioning is to give the overall SIZE dimensions of the scenic unit. This will incorporate all of the heights and widths. Be careful that all of your placement subtotal dimensions add up to the overall size total dimensions.

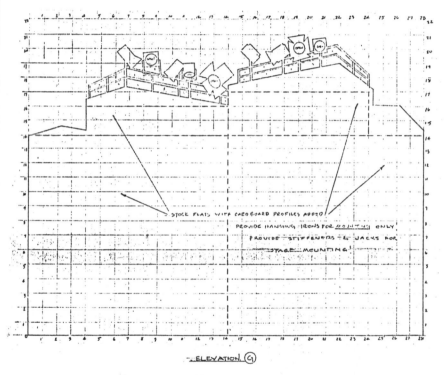

ELEVATION (G)

Occasionally you will encounter complicated and irregularly shaped scenic units such as a profile flat tree with its intricate branches and leaves. It is usually quite impossible to dimension these sorts of things in the standard way. In cases such as these it is best to grid the drawing with a 1' grid. The shop staff or scenic artist will then duplicate this grid at full scale in order to copy your drawing.

Another dimensioning feature that you will encounter and that we have not covered is platform and stair tread heights in a PLAN. These dimensions are placed inside a circle and are drawn in the center of the platform or tread. The dimension is written in inches (not feet and inches) from the stage floor with a plus sign in front of it. A four foot high platform dimension would read +48″. This is explained in more detail in the section on PLANS.

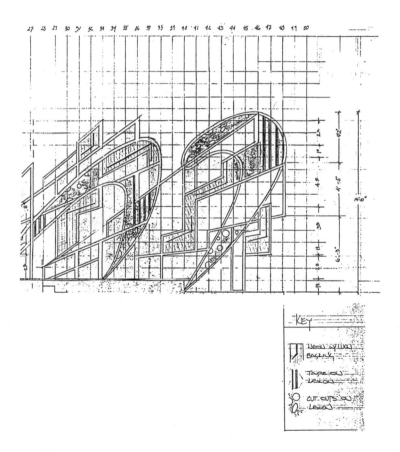

Gridded ELEVATIONS from *Top of the Pops* (Television).

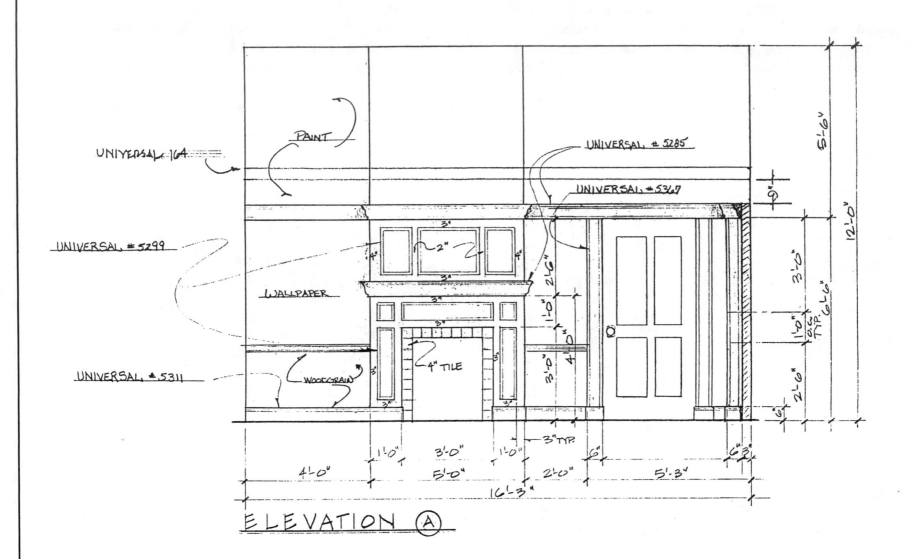

ELEVATION Ⓐ

Dimensioned <u>ELEVATION</u> for *The Boys* (Television).

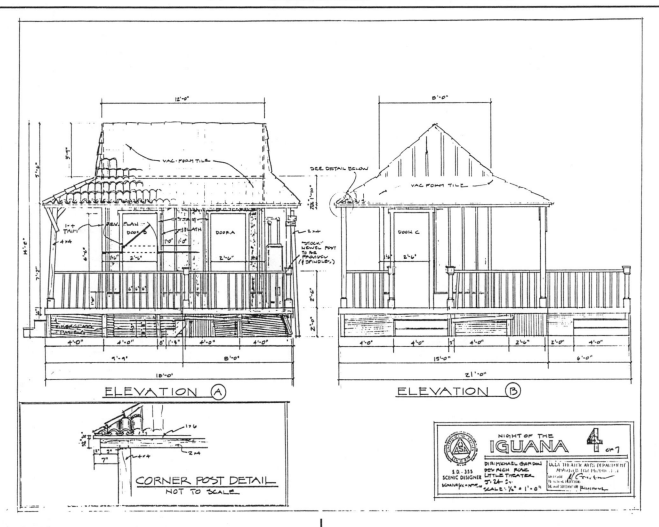

ELEVATIONS for *Night of the Iguana* (Theater).

Project 4   Dimensions

1. Draw a ¾″ border around your sheet.
2. Outline, in layout lines, the position of your title block.
3. Trace the drawing on the next sheet onto your drafting paper (centered).

4. Fully dimension the drawing. Round off to the nearest inch. Do not use fractions of an inch.
5. Complete your title block.

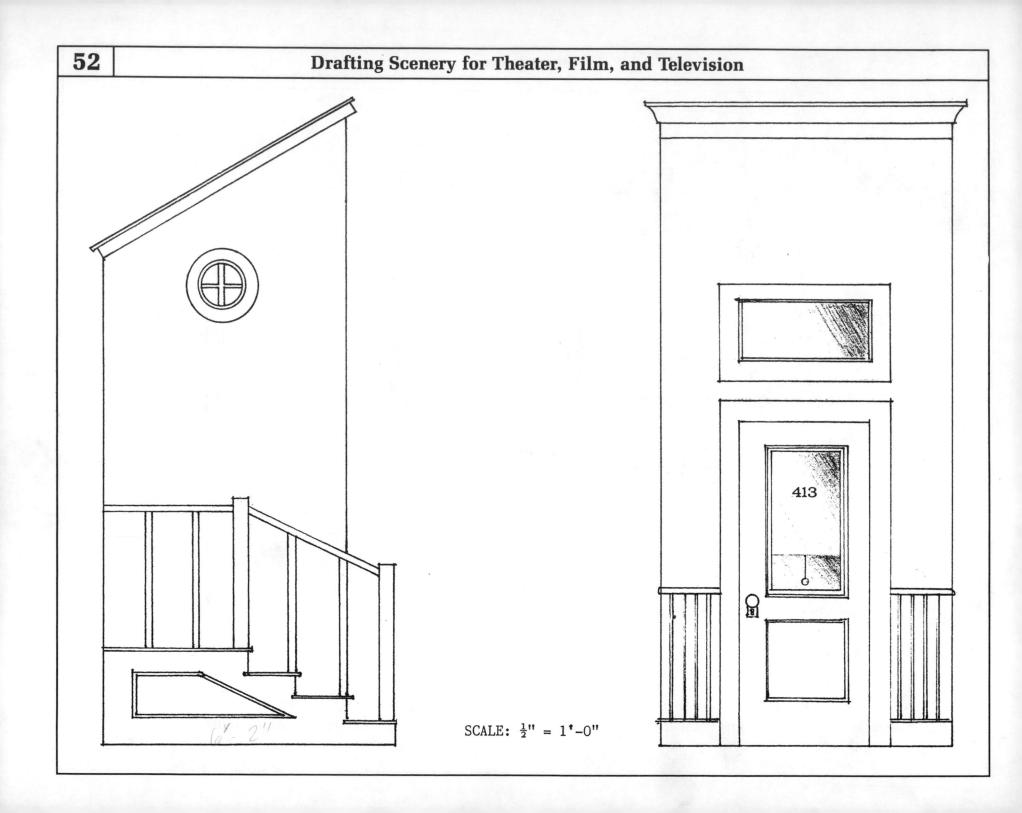

413

SCALE: $\frac{1}{2}$" = 1'-0"

6. Floor Plans and Staging Plans

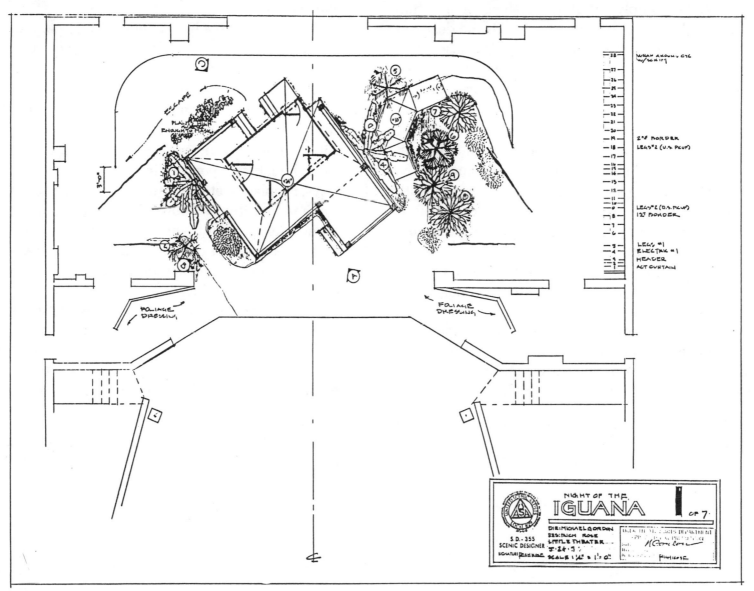

PLAN for *Night of the Iguana* (Theater).

The FLOOR PLAN is a road map of the performance space. In the theater it is sometimes referred to as a GROUND PLAN or simply a PLAN. In television and film it is usually called a STAGING PLAN. It aids the designer in developing the architecture of the setting. It is also a tool for the director to use in establishing the flow of the action. To the lighting designer it is a mandatory instrument for planning the lighting design. And for the stage technician it is invaluable regarding the placement of the scenery.

It is *not*, however, a plan from which to build. For instance the width of walls is not indicated on the PLAN. Construction information such as this is found in the ELEVATIONS section of the working drawings. Dimensions found on the PLAN are for the positioning of the set only and not the building of it.

FLOOR PLANS or STAGING PLANS are usually thought of as bird's eye views of the set on the stage. But it isn't quite that simple. If you really think about it, a bird's eye view would show you a bunch of roof mounted mechanical and air conditioning units. The PLAN is a bird's eye view of the set on stage after an imaginary line has been drawn 4′ from the stage floor all around the set and stage. Then an imaginary crew comes along with a circular saw, cuts along the line and removes everything above the mark.

None of this really happens, of course, but it is a good way to think of this drawing whether you are reading one or drawing one. So the PLAN is actually a "cut view" or horizontal section view of the set in place on stage. The imaginary cutting plane which we said was at 4′ actually varies in height in order to make the drawing clearer. It will go higher or lower than the 4′ in order to go through all architectural openings in the set walls: windows, doorways, fireplaces, etc. Another peculiarity about this cutting plane is that it goes above all platforms and stairways—it never cuts through them. Although these variations make the whole thing sound confusing, they occur so that a maximum amount of information about the scenery will be revealed on the drawing.

The effect that this variable cutting plane line has on the finished drawing is considerable:

a. All scenic elements that lie below this line including platforms, staircases, rugs, window sills, furniture, etc. are drawn in a medium-weight line.

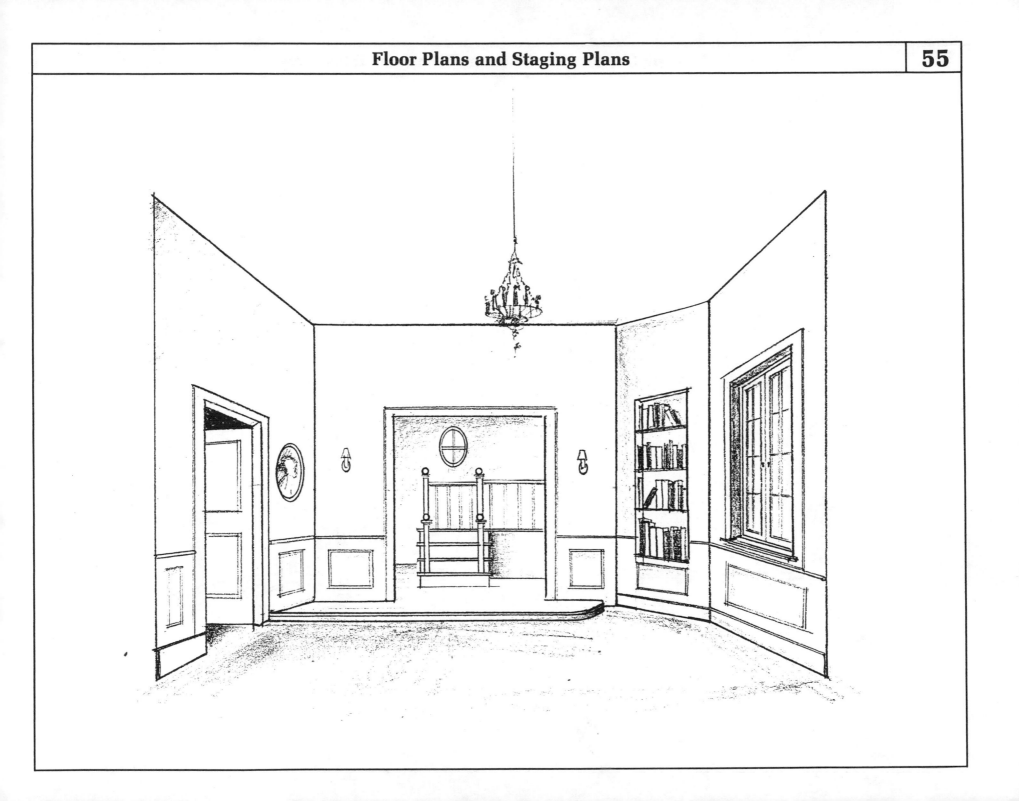

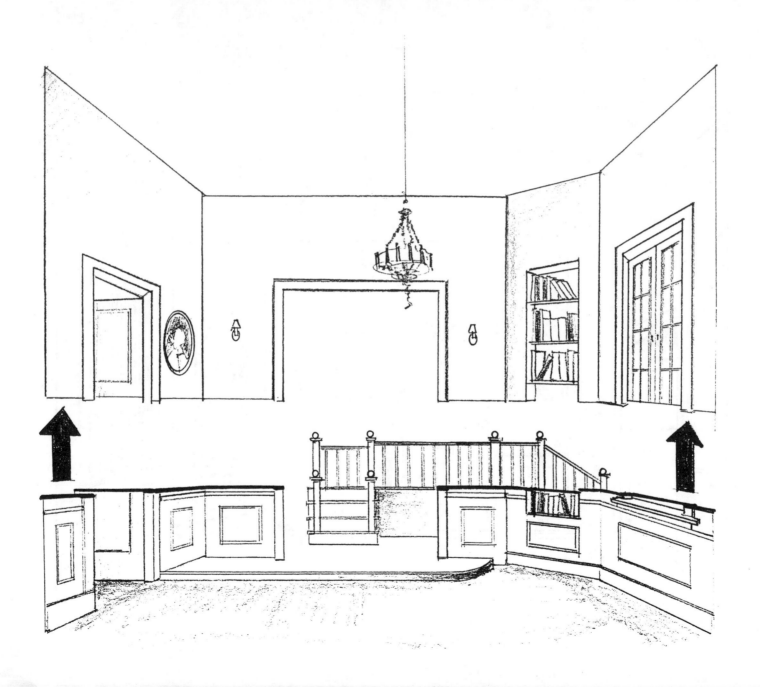

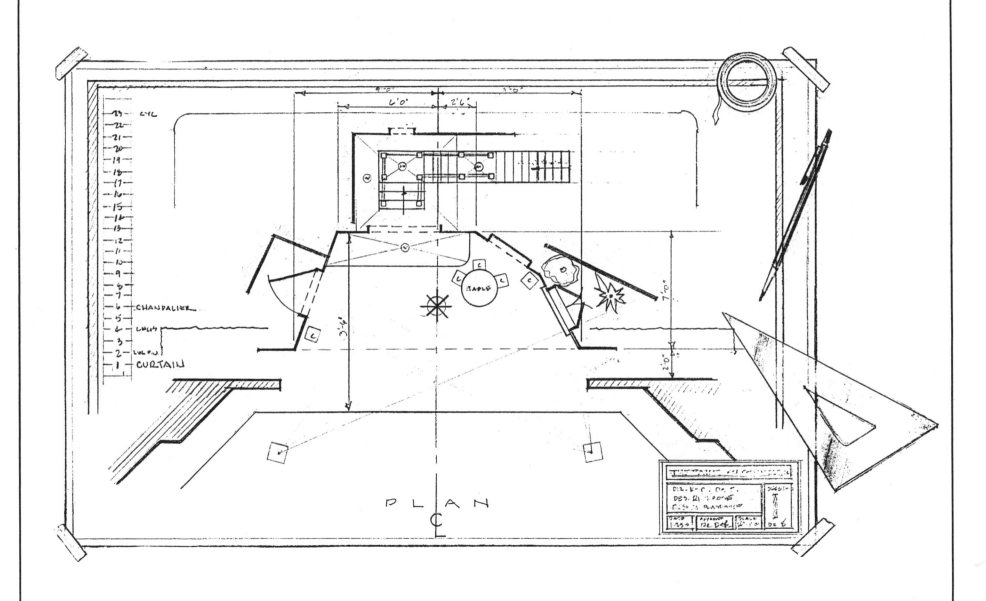

b. All scenery that lies above this line including ceilings, cornice moldings, skylights, drops, other flown scenery, etc. is drawn in a dashed line.

c. Any scenery actually "cut" by the line including walls, doors, windows, trees, masking drapery, etc. is drawn with a heavy-weight line.

These line variations result in an almost three-dimensional effect. It becomes instantly clear as to what is a wall and what is a platform. It's simple to determine what is on the deck and what is high above it—what are walls and what aren't.

PLAN views have a unique set of symbols which help communicate information graphically. Most of these symbols have a logical basis once you understand them. For instance the symbol for a doorway has two dashed lines going from side to side. Although it may seem cryptic at first, it really is quite rational. The dashed lines represent the thickness of the header which goes across the doorway. If you remember that anything in a PLAN above 4′ is dashed, this makes complete sense. The symbol for the platform, however, is another story. A rectangular platform is drawn with its four sides in a medium-weight line. But if you recall our rules about the cutting plane line, this could also mean four sticks on the stage floor! There wouldn't be any difference in the way you draw them. In order to make this look like a solid top, a platform symbol has two diagonal lines from each corner to its opposite corner, resulting in an X. In the middle of that X is a circle with the platform height in inches. A two foot high platform would read +24″. Not quite as logical as the doorway, but it does make sense once it is explained.

Here are some more examples of these symbols unique to the PLAN.

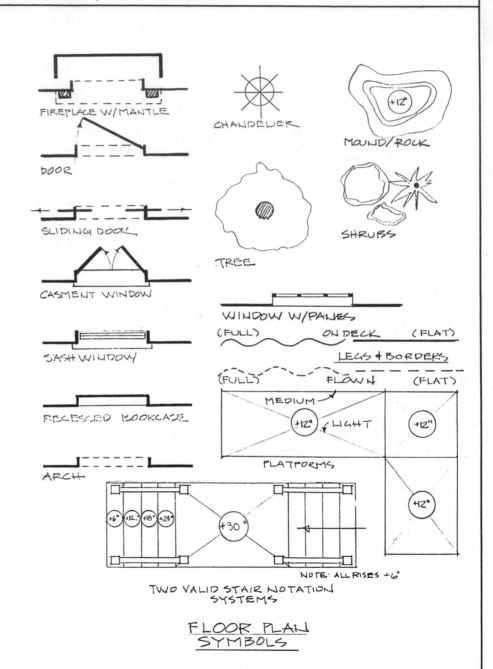

FIREPLACE W/MANTLE

DOOR

SLIDING DOOR

CASMENT WINDOW

SASH WINDOW

RECESSED BOOKCASE

ARCH

CHANDELIER

TREE

MOUND/ROCK

SHRUBS

WINDOW W/PANES
(FULL)   ON DECK   (FLAT)

LEGS & BORDERS
(FULL)   FLOWN   (FLAT)

PLATFORMS

NOTE: ALL RISES +6″

TWO VALID STAIR NOTATION SYSTEMS

FLOOR PLAN SYMBOLS

Getting Started on a <u>FLOOR PLAN</u>— Theater (Proscenium)

1. Tape a blueprint or photocopy of the theater to your drafting table. Make sure that the horizontal and vertical lines on the copy line up with the arms of your drafting machine.

2. Attach your vellum to the table right over the copy of the theater or stage.

Many draftspersons prefer to apply drafting powder before drawing the first line of any drafting. Drafting powder is a rubbery dust that is sprinkled from a can or squeezed from a little bag. It does two things to keep the drawing and the drafting instruments cleaner and more smudge free. First, the particles are like little erasers rolling around constantly erasing the lightest of smudges. Second, the particles act like little ball bearings which force the drafting instruments to glide just above the surface of the paper eliminating the source of most smudges. The powder can be a nuisance if applied too liberally. As the pencil hits each particle it causes a skip in the line resulting in a page full of dashed lines. Use it sparingly to avoid this effect.

3. Find the critical seats in the theater. These are the seats furthest away from the center line in the front and back rows. Sometimes these seats are found a few rows further back than the front row.

4. In layout weight line, draw the eight sightlines from the critical seats. Each sightline begins at the center of the seat, intersects with the onstage side of the proscenium opening (S.R.) and continues until it hits the back wall of the theater. The second sightline from that seat does the same thing except that it intersects with the other side of the proscenium opening (S.L.).

The set should be placed in the common sightline area of the stage. That is, no part of the set should go beyond (offstage) any of the sightlines drawn in step 4. If it does, that part of the set will not be seen by certain areas of the audience.

5. Find the center line on the blueprint and draw it on your vellum. The center line is a special line used to indicate the midway point in the proscenium opening. It runs from the top of the drawing to the bottom. At the bottom it is finished off with an overlapping CL (see example).

6. In layout weight line draw a horizontal line from the locking rail all the way across the stage representing the position of where the act curtain, fire curtain, or any downstage drops might fall. These are determining factors in limiting the downstage position of any scenery.

7. Draw the set walls, platforms, stairways, etc. on the stage. Be sure that you follow the rules regarding line weights and the rules of the cutting plane.

8. Dimension the set so that it can be accurately positioned during the load-in phase. This is done by drawing dimension lines from some key corners (at least 4) of the set to known architectural features (including the centerline) of the theater or stage. It's important to understand that you need to give both a vertical and horizontal dimension for each corner to "nail it" accurately.

9. Indicate the alternate position (on or off stage) of any scenery which is mobile (special light-weight dashed lines).

10. Draw and label all furniture, rugs, etc.

11. Draw all drops, cycs, scrims, and other masking in heavy-weight line (see MASKING THE STAGE).

12. Label all flying pieces by identifying them next to the counterweight line set that they fly on.

13. Draw your title block in the lower right-hand corner.

14. Draw in the architecture of the theater.

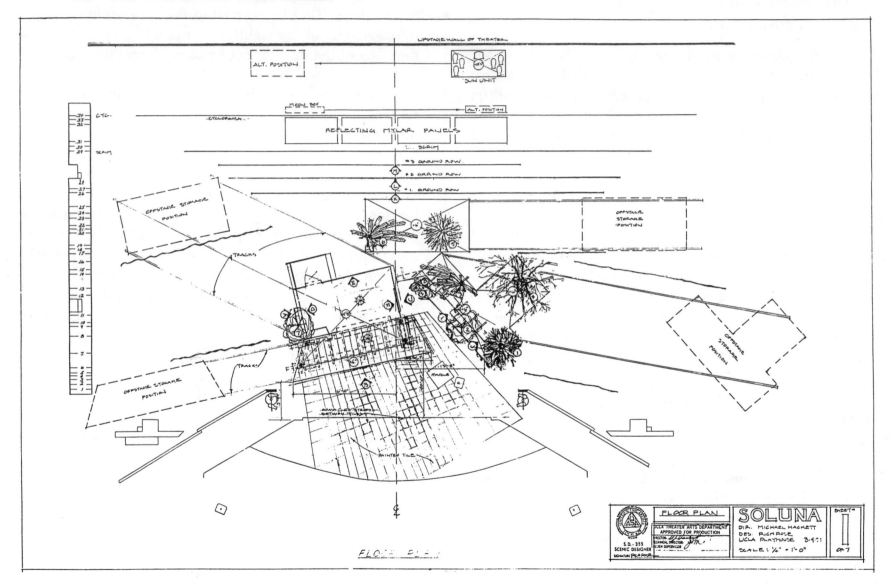

PLAN for *Soluna* showing track positions for moving
platforms (Theater).

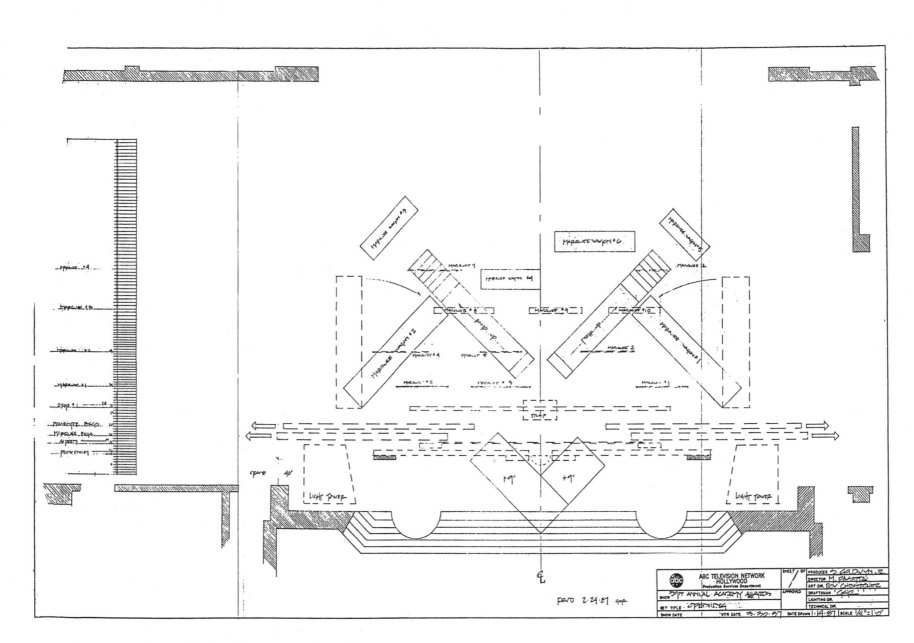

FLOOR PLAN for 59th Academy Awards (Television).

Getting Started on a <u>STAGING PLAN</u>— Television/Film

1. Tape a blueprint or photocopy of the stage to your drafting table. Make sure that the horizontal and vertical lines on the copy line up with the arms of your drafting machine.

2. Attach your vellum to the table right over the copy of the theater or stage.

Many draftspersons prefer to apply drafting powder before drawing the first line of any drafting. Drafting powder is a rubbery dust that is sprinkled from a can or squeezed from a little bag. It does two things to keep the drawing and the drafting instruments cleaner and more smudge free. First, the particles are like little erasers rolling around constantly erasing the lightest of smudges. Second, the particles act like little ball bearings which force the drafting instruments to glide just above the surface of the paper eliminating the source of most smudges. The powder can be a nuisance if applied too liberally. As the pencil hits each particle it causes a skip in the line resulting in a page full of dashed lines. Use it sparingly to avoid this effect.

3. In layout weight line, draw the stage perimeter fire clearance line. This is usually a line 4′ from the edge of any wall or obstruction all around the studio. No scenery is allowed to violate this line.

4. If there is a studio audience, position the audience seating bleachers. Be sure to allow for all access stairs to and from all sections of the bleachers.

5. If there is to be an audience, find out where they will enter and exit. This area needs to remain clear and should look tidy.

6. If this is a multi-camera video tape, lay out where the camera pedestal/microphone dolly lane will be. This needs to be 14′ wide minimum. Anything narrower will not allow the equipment to pass each other between shots or scenes.

7. If there is an audience, some masking may be important. Traditional theatrical masking is not needed. However, sometimes a border is hung to hide any lights that might be annoying to the audience. If the sound of the audience is important, sets or actors may need to be hidden so as to avoid revealing any plot or other surprises during the taping. In these situations, act curtains are rigged on a counterweight or simple two-fold flats can be set up.

8. In layout weight line draw a horizontal line from the locking rail all the way across the stage representing the position of where the act curtain, fire curtain, or any downstage drops might fall. These are determining factors in limiting the downstage position of any scenery.

9. Draw the set walls, platforms, stairways, etc. on the stage. Be sure that you follow the rules regarding line weights and the rules of the cutting plane.

10. Indicate the alternate position (on or off stage) of any scenery which is mobile (special light-weight dashed lines).

11. Draw and label all furniture, rugs, etc.

12. Draw all drops, cycs, scrims, and other masking in heavy-weight line (see MASKING THE STAGE).

13. Label all flying pieces by identifying them next to the counterweight line set that they fly on.

14. Draw your title block in the lower right-hand corner. Be sure to include set-up and "on camera" dates.

15. Draw in the architecture of the studio or sound stage.

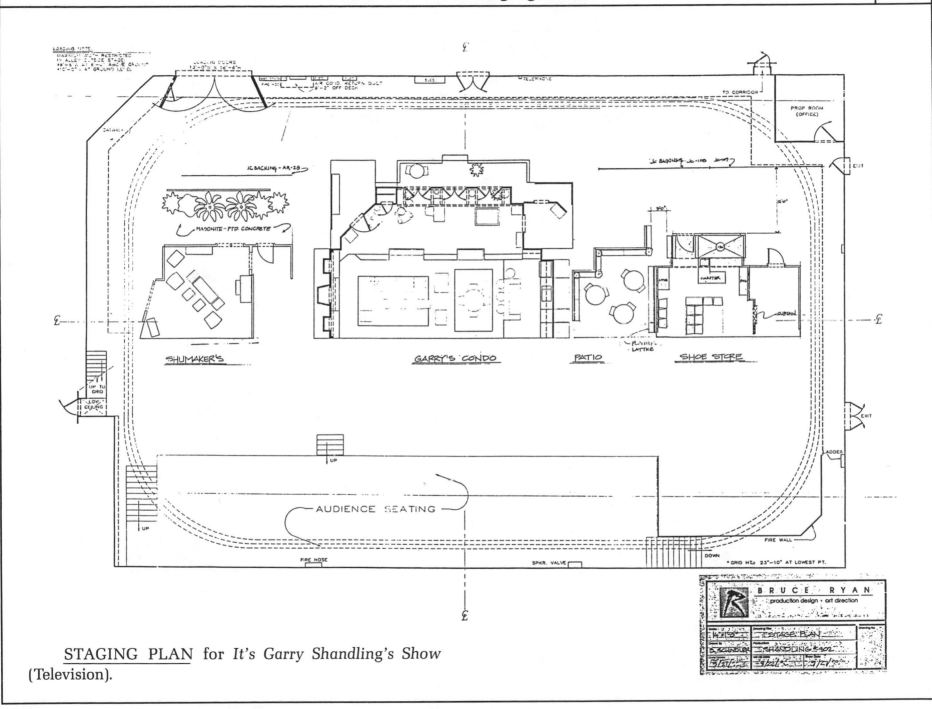

STAGING PLAN for *It's Garry Shandling's Show*
(Television).

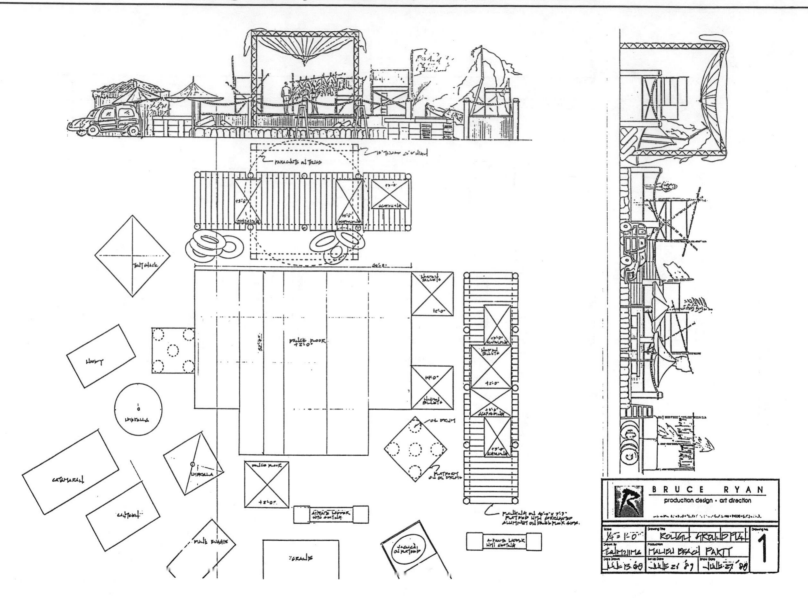

STAGING PLAN for *Malibu Beach Party* (Television).
Notice the use of ELEVATIONS on the same sheet developed directly from the PLAN.

Masking the Stage—Proscenium Theater

In most situations you will need to mask the offstage parts of the stage from the audience. Right now we'll discuss the masking that hides the wings from the audience. The fly space above, which also needs to be masked, will be covered in the section on CENTER LINE VERTICAL SECTIONS. We'll cover the traditional masking method of symmetrical, parallel legs (tormentors). Many masking variations exist but they are all variations on this tried and true technique.

You must approach the masking process as if there were no set at all on stage. Don't let your critical and adjusted sightlines be stopped by the set walls when calculating your masking positions. Although this sounds illogical, it really isn't. You see, the audience can look above the set walls and on out to the stage walls. If you approach the process thinking that the set will mask most of the stage you will only be half right—the bottom half.

1. Draw in all legs using heavy-weight (extra thick) lines. As a first rule of thumb, place the legs as far apart as possible. This will cause you to use the fewest number possible. The less cloth there is hanging offstage to catch the light, the better the stage picture will look. As a second rule of thumb, the onstage edge of the legs should line up with the line of the proscenium opening. This ensures that all of the audience sees about the same thing. Place them further offstage if possible, but never further onstage unless absolutely necessary.

2. Let's draw the first leg. Draw a layout line from the proscenium opening on stage right to the back wall of the theater. Let's call this line the *onstage* masking limit. This line is parallel to the center line.

3. Draw another line parallel to the onstage masking limit line. This line will be offstage of that line the distance of the width of the masking. We'll call this the *offstage* masking limit line.

4. Now draw a layout line that goes from the counterweight line set where the first leg will be and continues all the way across the stage.

HELP! How do you know where the first leg will be? Easy—it will be where the critical sightline from the opposite side of the audience crosses the *offstage* masking limit line. If there is no counterweight line set on line with that intersection, or it is already reserved for something else, then put this first leg on the closest downstage line set available. Never go upstage of a sightline to place your leg.

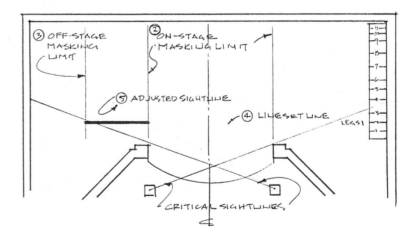

5. After you have drawn the first leg you need to draw an adjusted sightline. This line goes from the first row seat on the opposite side of the audience, intersects with the onstage edge of the first leg and continues on until it hits the side wall of the theater.

6. Now draw your second leg using the steps outlined above. After each leg is drawn you draw a new adjusted sightline from the first row seat. Only then can you draw a third and any subsequent legs.

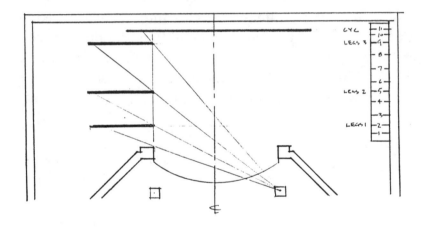

The position of each leg should be determined by:
—The two rules of thumb above.
—The first row critical or adjusted sightline hitting the onstage edge of each leg.
—The need to mask everything off stage and yet allow for scenery or actors to move freely.

7. Identify what is on each line set.

8. Analyze the position of the set on the stage. Make sure that the audience sees all that it is supposed to see and nothing else.

9. If there is to be any floor side lighting (trees, booms, shin busters, etc.) make sure that they are masked properly.

10. Reverse and repeat the masking for the other side of the stage.

11. Erase all "masking limit lines" and any other layout lines that might be confusing if blueprinted.

FLOOR PLAN Checklist—Theater

Use this checklist to be sure that you are including the necessary information in your FLOOR PLAN.
- [ ] ¾″ border around your sheet.
- [ ] Stage architecture drawn including:
  locking or pin rail
  catwalks
  overhangs or structures which might obstruct the movement of scenery or position of masking
  extreme sightline seats
- [ ] Sightlines drawn.
- [ ] Center-line drawn.
- [ ] All walls and platforms drawn.
- [ ] Any braces or jacks that hold up scenery are drawn in.
- [ ] Sightlines checked for scenery coverage through windows, doors, etc.
- [ ] Reveals and backings drawn.
- [ ] Set position dimensioned.
- [ ] Alternate moving scenery positions drawn.
- [ ] Furniture drawn and labeled.
- [ ] Door swings shown.
- [ ] Platform and stair heights indicated.
- [ ] Floor openings (traps) noted.

☐ Overhead scenery drawn including:
ceilings
cornices
beams
chandeliers
flying scenic units
☐ Masking drawn including:
cyclorama
scrims
drops
tormentors or legs
teasers or borders
☐ Sightlines checked again for coverage.
☐ Line sets labeled.
☐ Title block drawn in lower right corner.

STAGING PLAN Checklist—Television/Film

Use this checklist to be sure that you are including the necessary information in your STAGING PLAN.
☐ ¾″ border around your sheet.
☐ Stage architecture drawn including:
locking or pin rail
catwalks
overhangs or structures which might obstruct the movement of scenery or position of masking
extreme sightline seats
☐ 4′ fire clearance line drawn.
☐ 14′ camera/microphone dolly lane drawn.
☐ Audience bleachers drawn.
☐ Bleacher access stairs drawn.
☐ Audience entrance kept clear.
☐ All walls and platforms drawn.
☐ Any braces or jacks that hold up scenery are drawn in.

☐ Reveals and backings drawn.
☐ Alternate moving scenery positions drawn.
☐ Furniture drawn and labeled.
☐ Door swings shown.
☐ Platform and stair heights indicated.
☐ Floor openings (traps) noted.
☐ Overhead scenery drawn including:
ceilings
cornices
beams
chandeliers
flying scenic units
☐ Masking drawn including:
cyclorama
scrims
drops
tormentors or borders
☐ Line sets labeled.
☐ Title block drawn in lower right corner.

Project 5   FLOOR PLANS

1. Obtain a blueprint or photocopy of a proscenium theater on which to draw a FLOOR PLAN.

2. Translate the roughly sketched floor plan on the next page into a neat, finished FLOOR PLAN. This should be a complete PLAN that includes all stairs, escapes, scenery, and masking.

3. Note that the information is sketched to no scale and that much of it is missing.

4. The masking inventory is limitless. However, all legs (tormentors) are 10′ wide. The width of all other drops, scrims, etc. is to be determined by you.

5. Be sure to include a title block and the theater archi-

tecture in your drawing. Use the steps outlined in this
section on <u>FLOOR PLANS</u> as a guide to completing this
project.

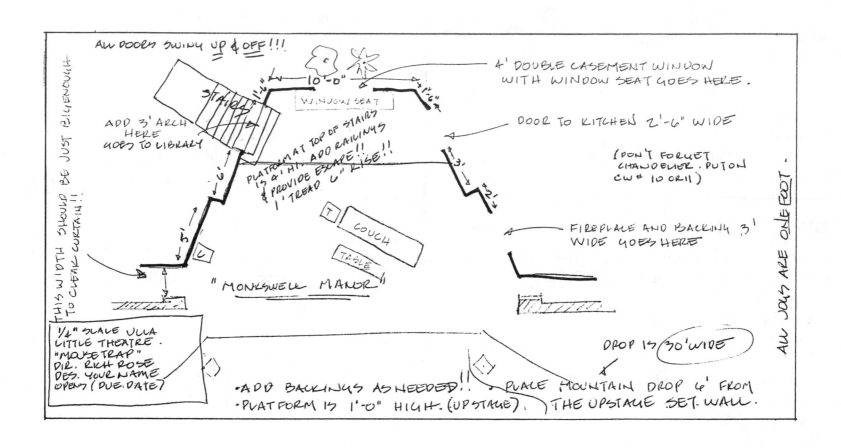

7. Platform Plans

Once the configuration of the FLOOR PLAN or STAGING PLAN has been agreed to by the producer, director, and designers you can begin work on the construction drawing phase of the plans. The first of these drawings is the PLATFORM PLAN. The PLATFORM PLAN is similar to a FLOOR PLAN in that it is a plan view of the performance space, but at the same time it is much more specialized. While the FLOOR PLAN is a picture of all scenery and masking on the deck, the PLATFORM PLAN shows only the platforms and stair units—close up and in detail. This drawing shows no walls, masking, or other non-platform related information.

The primary function of the PLATFORM PLAN is to communicate much of the information needed for the construction of the platform and stair units; information regarding placement of these units is secondary. If possible, the PLATFORM PLAN should be drawn in ½" scale. A smaller scale would be too small to convey the information and contain the accuracy required. If necessary, draw this ½" PLAN in two parts on two sheets.

The PLATFORM PLAN shows in detail:

1. PLATFORM BREAKDOWN—When a large platform, such as 16' × 20', is specified for a production, it may actually be made up of smaller platforms from a "stock" inventory. Such inventories as these are usually made up of a large number of 4' × 8' platforms. These smaller platforms are combined to make up the larger platform. Rather than show one large platform, this particular PLATFORM PLAN would indicate 10 smaller 4' × 8' platforms. Stock units should be labeled with the word "STOCK" on it, and units to be built should be labeled "TO BE BUILT."

Even if the platform is being built without a stock inventory, it is a good idea to designate how you want the 4' × 8' sheets of plywood and/or Masonite which make up the tops of the platforms arrayed.

2. CONSTRUCTION DETAIL—Such details would include: platform material (wood, steel, scaffold), surfacing material (Masonite, plywood, ground cloth, carpet), acoustical considerations (sound deadening board above the plywood and below a Masonite top surface, "stuffing" material below the platforms to eliminate a hollow sound), method of joining platforms to each other, facing materials, method of legging platforms up to desired height, etc.

3. FLOOR OPENINGS—Any openings in the platforms or openings in the stage floor itself (traps) must be indicated and fully dimensioned. If there are any escape stairs down through the traps they too must be drawn, positioned, and dimensioned. A separate BELOW STAGE PLATFORM PLAN may be necessary.

4. DIMENSIONS—You need full dimensioning indicating widths and lengths as well as heights of all of the individual platforms that make up the larger platform. Also included here would be the overall size of the large platform. If possible, it is also a good idea to indicate the position of the platforms on the stage. This should be done in the same way that you positioned your FLOOR PLAN with

dimensions. A center line and edge of stage, or other architectural element, should be included to anchor the dimensions. Remember that each positioning dimension must have both a horizontal and vertical dimension to "nail it down."

5. RADII OF CURVED PLATFORMS—Not only should the radius be dimensioned but also the center of the radius needs to be located and dimensioned.

6. CASTER INFORMATION—If the platforms roll (wagons) you need to:

    a. indicate swivel or rigid casters.

    b. convey the diameter of the wheel and the overall caster height.

c. point out the placement of each caster on each platform. If the caster is rigid yet the platform moves in an arc (jackknife platform) you need to indicate the angle at which each caster must be mounted underneath the platform (hidden line).

d. identify and position with dimensions the location of any platform pivot point.

7. TRACKING INFORMATION—Any method that you or the designer have in mind for the control and tracking of any wagons, turntables, jackknife stages, etc. must be drawn in and specified. All tracks, position of tracks, and position of control devices (cable, pulleys, motors, etc.) must be fully dimensioned.

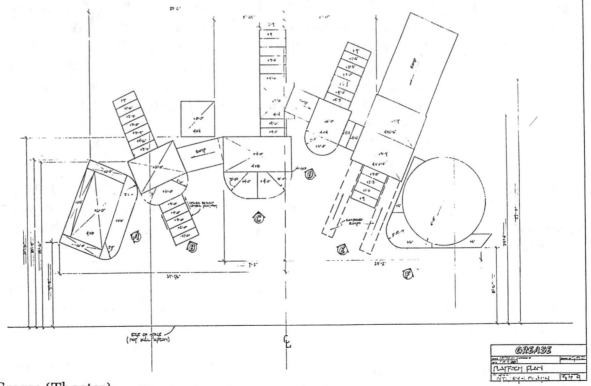

PLATFORM PLAN for *Grease* (Theater).

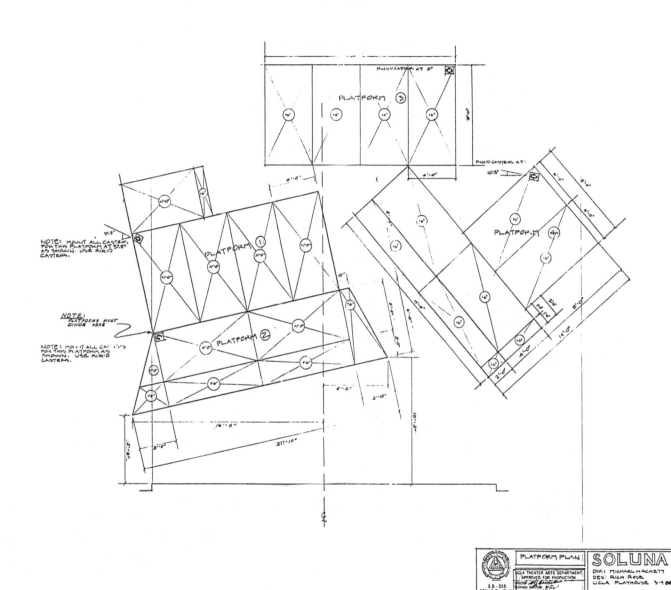

PLATFORM PLAN

SOLUNA

DIR: MICHAEL HACKETT
DES: RICH ROSE
UCLA PLAYHOUSE 5-9-80

SHEET: 3 OF 7

UCLA THEATER ARTS DEPARTMENT
APPROVED FOR PRODUCTION

SCENIC DESIGNER

SCALE: ½" = 1'-0"

PLATFORM PLAN for *Soluna* (Theater).

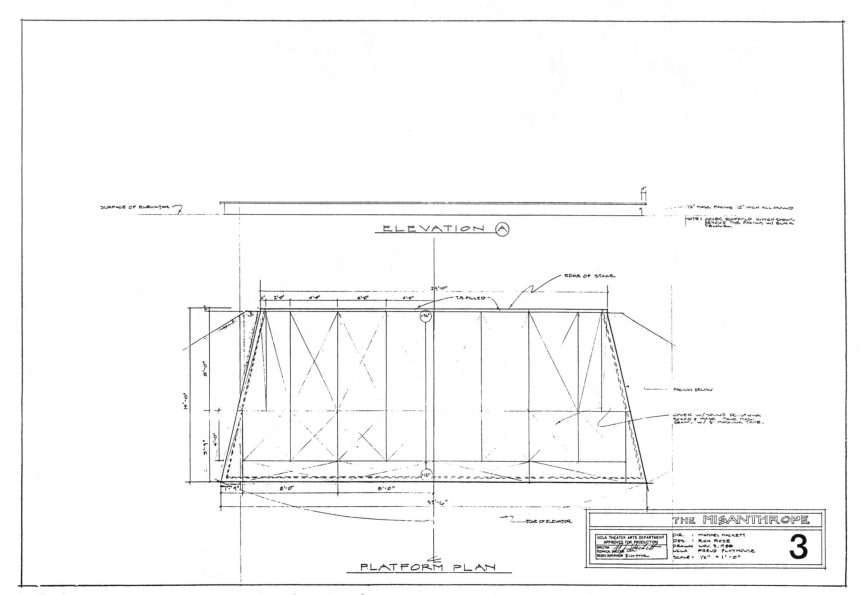

Raked stage <u>PLATFORM PLAN</u> for *The Misanthrope* (Theater).

Checklist

Use this checklist to be sure that you are including the necessary information on your PLATFORM PLAN.

- [ ] ¾″ border around the sheet
- [ ] Edge of stage drawn (or other permanent architectural features to be used for dimensioning purposes)
- [ ] Center line drawn
- [ ] All platforms and stair units drawn
- [ ] Platform breakdown into smaller stock units completed
- [ ] Platform joining technique included
- [ ] Platform legging technique included
- [ ] Platform construction technique included
- [ ] Platform surface materials and techniques included
- [ ] Platforms fully dimensioned
- [ ] Platform heights indicated
- [ ] Radii of all curved platforms included and centers of all radii dimensioned
- [ ] Casters specified and positions plotted
- [ ] Tracks and control devices drawn, specified, and dimensioned
- [ ] Placement of the platforms on the stage in relation to the edge of the stage and to the center line dimensioned
- [ ] Floor openings noted
- [ ] Title block drawn

Project 6   PLATFORM PLANS

1. Draw a border around your sheet.
2. Lay out the position of your title block.
3. Draw a PLATFORM PLAN for the FLOOR PLAN on the next page.
4. The FLOOR PLAN is drawn in ⅛″ scale. Draw your PLATFORM PLAN in ½″ scale. Break down the platforms using the inventory indicated below.
5. Finish your title block.

INVENTORY
3 4′ × 8′ platforms (6 inches high)
1 1′ × 8′ platform (6 inches high)
1 1′ × 4′ platform (6 inches high)

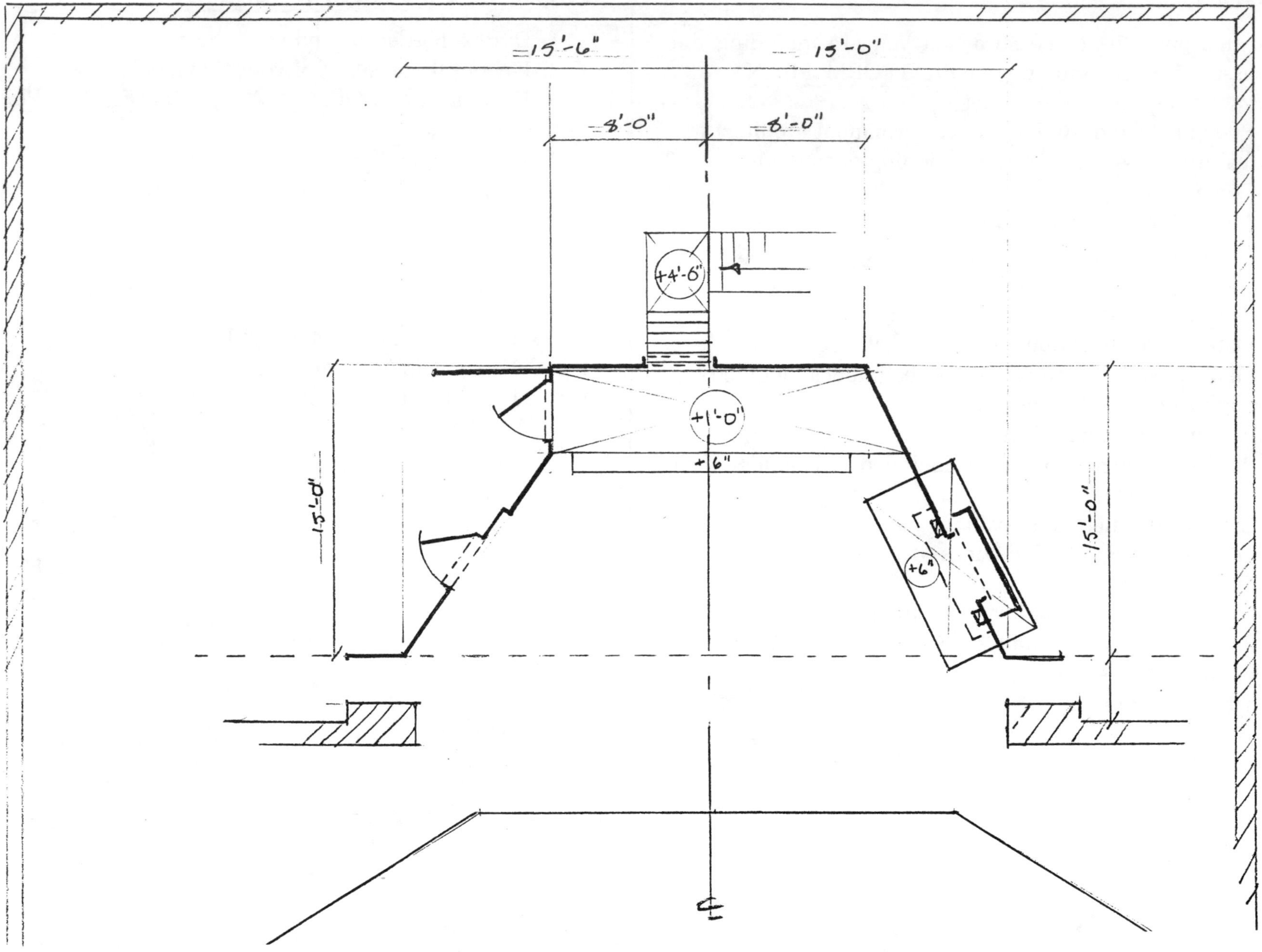

15'-6" 15'-0"

8'-0" 8'-0"

+4'-6"

+1'-0"

+6"

15'-0" 15'-0"

+6"

℄

8. Elevations

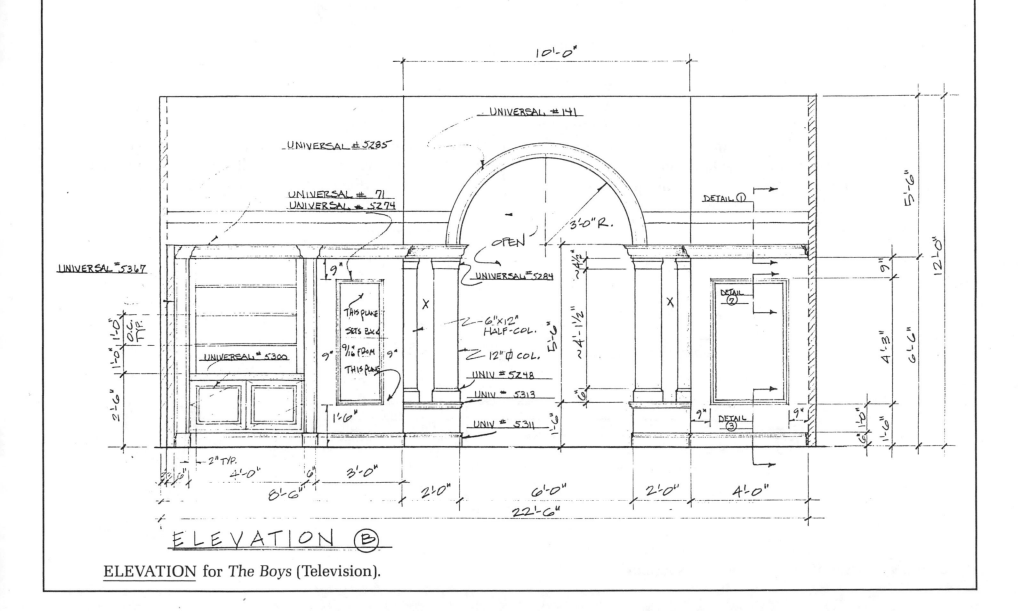

ELEVATION Ⓑ

ELEVATION for *The Boys* (Television).

The next classification of drafting undertaken in the working drawings is the ELEVATION drawings. ELEVATIONS show either the front, back, or side of a particular portion of the FLOOR PLAN and "elevate" it into a straight on, flattened out, full face, no perspective view of that part of the set (whether from the front, side, or rear). It should contain all of the structural information needed to build that piece of scenery and all of the applied or painted detail (moldings, trims, windows, etc.) that will eventually be a part of that scenery. The outline of the structure and all of the detail are drawn in a medium-weight .5mm line.

Some scenery is more routine, normal, or typical than others. An example might be a common muslin flat with some molding attached to it for a Victorian interior box set. In a case such as this, one FRONT ELEVATION will do fine to explain the construction. Your scene shop has built thousands of muslin flats and does not need a REAR ELEVATION to be shown how to do so.

Sometimes it is not possible to convey all the pertinent information in a FRONT ELEVATION. Or perhaps the scenery uses a special construction technique or maybe it is quite complicated. In these cases, before moving on to the next piece of scenery, the FRONT ELEVATION must be augmented with one or more additional drawings such as a SIDE ELEVATION, REAR ELEVATION, and/or DETAIL drawings done in the same or larger scale.

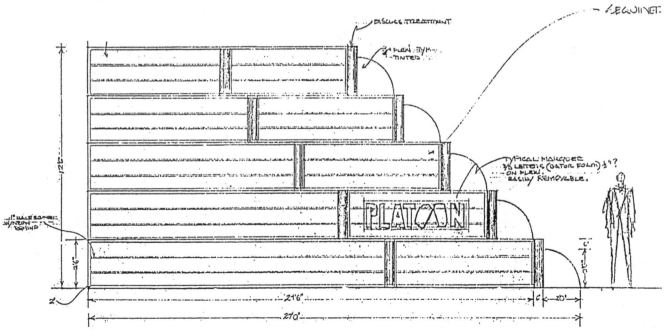

ELEVATION from Academy Awards (Television) including a human figure conveying a sense of scale.

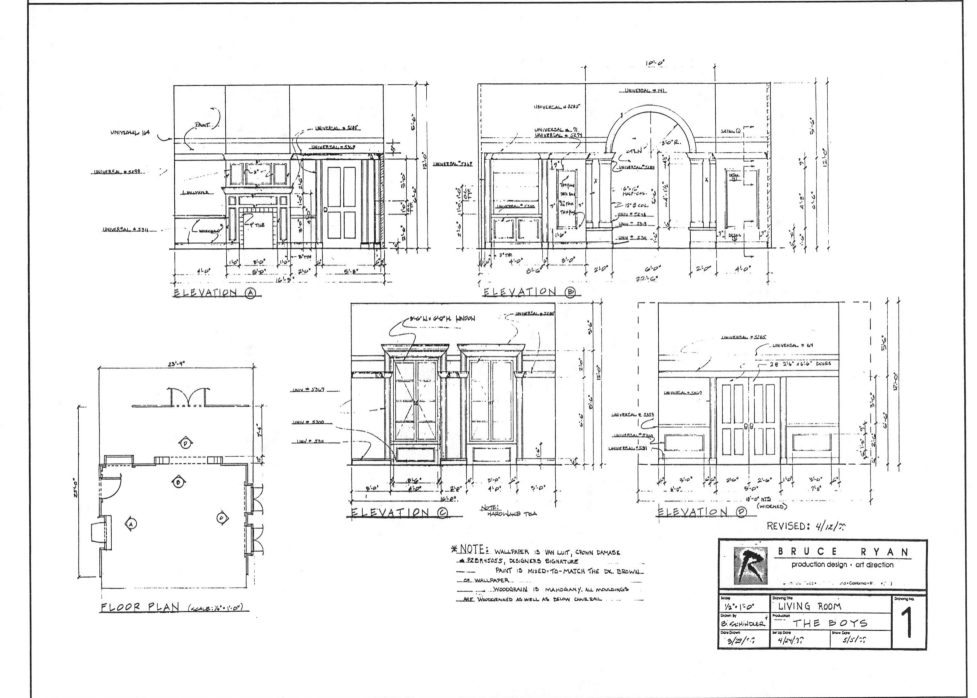

ELEVATION Ⓐ

ELEVATION Ⓑ

ELEVATION Ⓒ

NOTE: HARDWARE TBA

ELEVATION Ⓓ

FLOOR PLAN (SCALE: ¼" = 1'-0")

REVISED: 4/12/??

✳ NOTE: WALLPAPER IS VAN LUIT, CROWN DAMASK
PZB4505S, DESIGNERS SIGNATURE
PAINT IS MIXED-TO-MATCH THE DK. BROWN
OF WALLPAPER
WOODGRAIN IS MAHOGANY. ALL MOULDINGS
ARE WOODGRAINED AS WELL AS BELOW CHAIR RAIL

BRUCE RYAN
production design · art direction

Scale	Drawing Title	
½" = 1'-0"	LIVING ROOM	Drawing No.
Drawn By	Production	
B. SCHINDLER	THE BOYS	**1**
Date Drawn	Set Up Date	Show Date
3/29/??	4/24/??	5/5/??

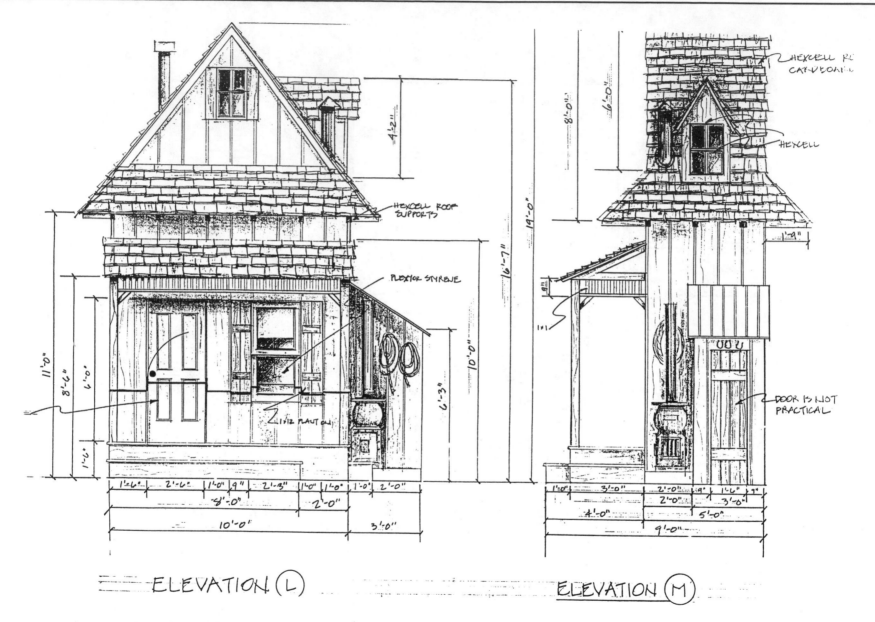

ELEVATION (L)

ELEVATION (M)

ELEVATIONS for *Oklahoma!* (Theater). The rendering-like quality of the **ELEVATIONS** can help the carpenters with the feel of the piece.

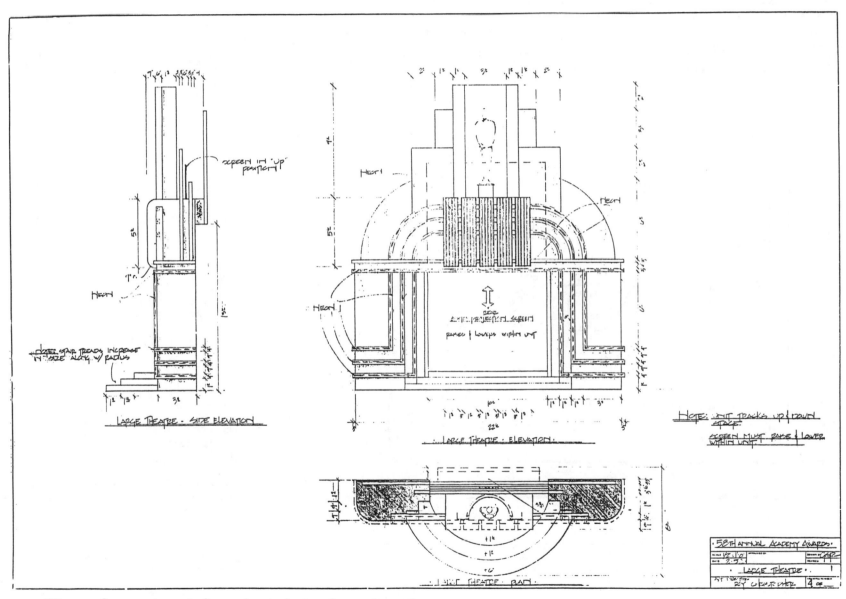

Views of a scenic unit from the 58th Academy Awards
('Television). Notice the extensive use of the "TV" dimensioning system.

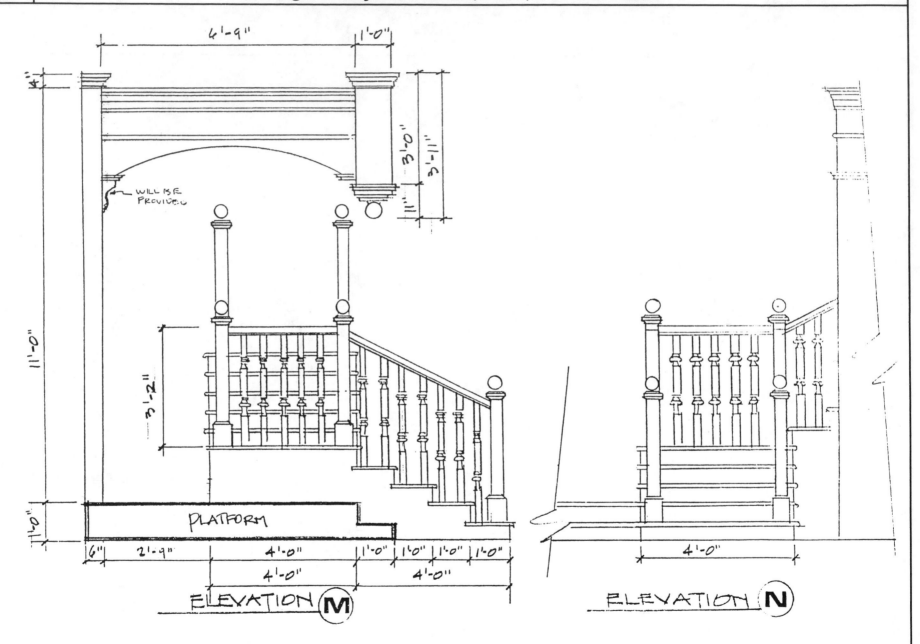

ELEVATION (M)

ELEVATION (N)

Intricate molding in <u>ELEVATIONS</u> such as spindle turnings can present quite a challenge.

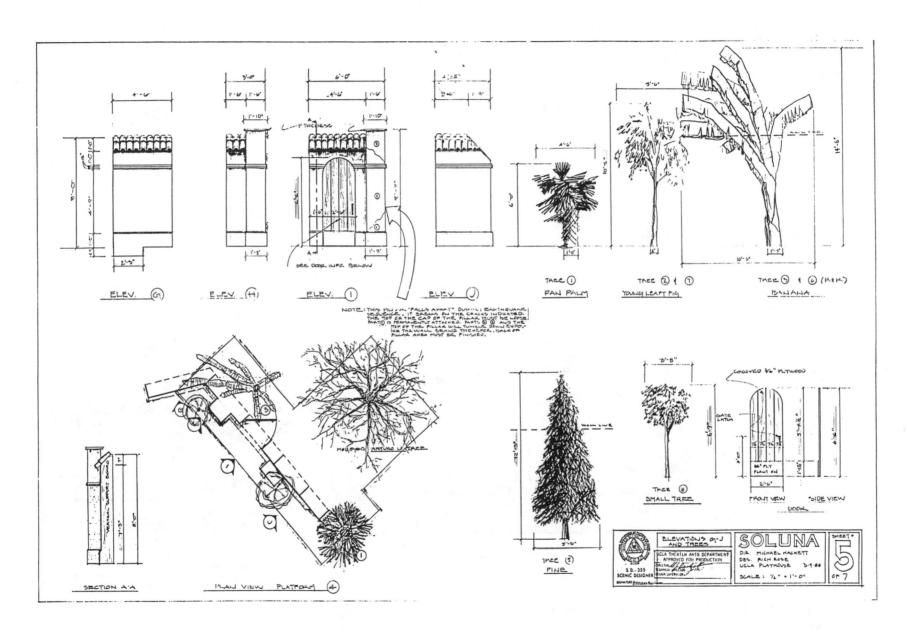

ELEVATIONS which include a **PLAN** for reference.

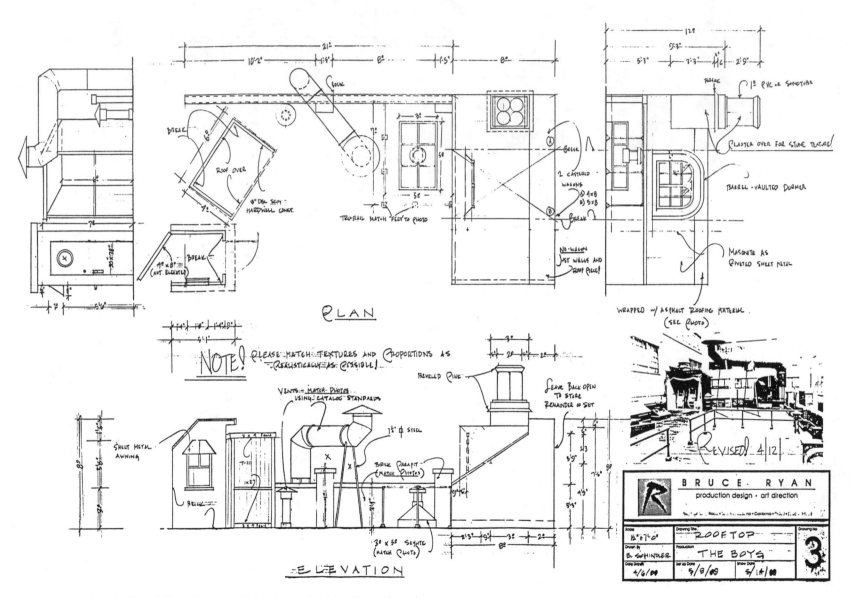

PLAN

ELEVATION

ELEVATIONS for *The Boys* (Television) developed from **PLAN**. Notice the acetate research photo attached to the drawing and blueprinted.

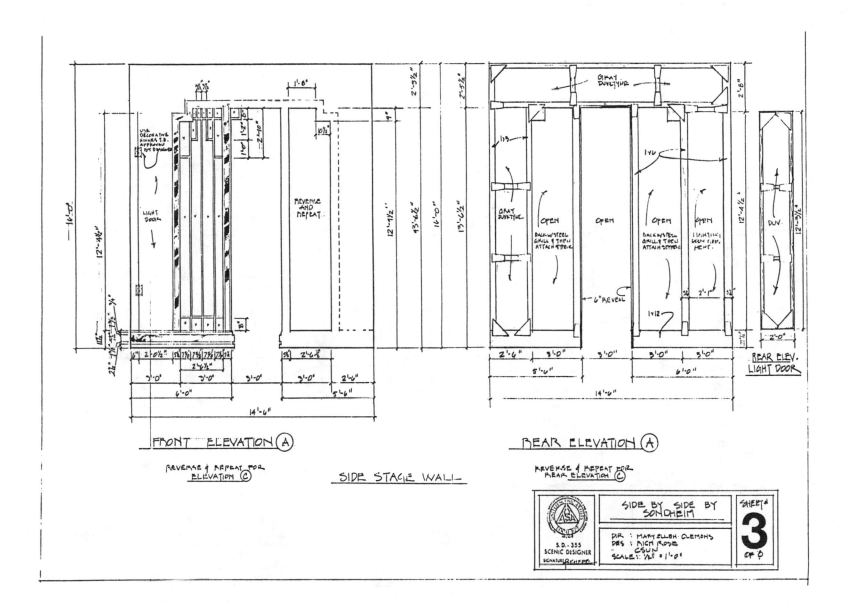

FRONT ELEVATION (A)

REVERSE & REPEAT FOR
ELEVATION (C)

SIDE STAGE WALL

REAR ELEVATION (A)

REVERSE & REPEAT FOR
REAR ELEVATION (C)

REAR ELEV.
LIGHT DOOR

SIDE BY SIDE BY
SONDHEIM

SHEET # 3 OF 8

DIR : MARYELLEN CLEMONS
DES : RICH ROSE
        CSUN
SCALE : 1/2" = 1'-0"

S.D. - 355
SCENIC DESIGNER
SIGNATURE R. Rose

FRONT and REAR ELEVATIONS for *Side by Side
by Sondheim* (Theater).

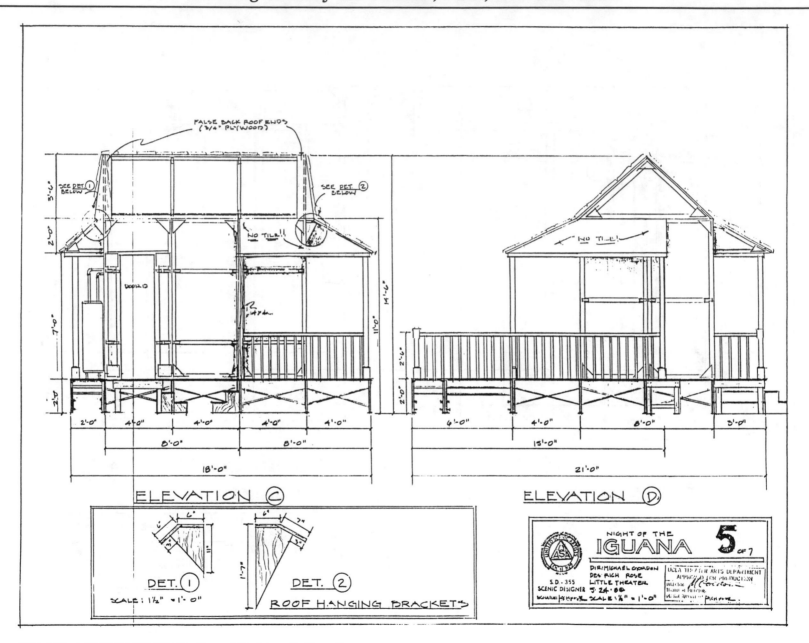

REAR ELEVATIONS for *Night of the Iguana* (Theater).

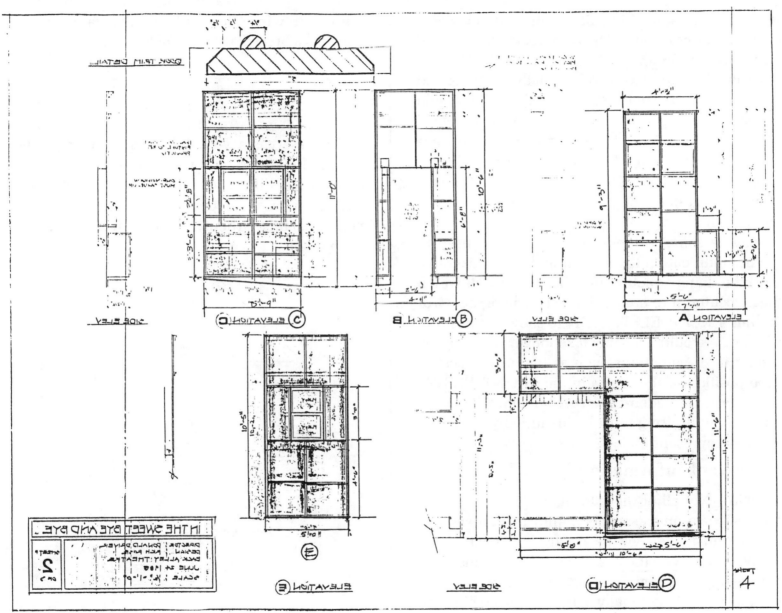

REAR ELEVATIONS of hard-wall construction flats.
These ELEVATIONS were drawn on a brown-line print of
the FRONT ELEVATION and then blueprinted.

If the scenery is something like a three-dimensional oddly shaped wall covered with foam rocks, you would also need to draw CONSTRUCTION ELEVATIONS that visually explain all of the steps involved in the building and assembly. Whereas a normal FRONT ELEVATION would show the outer surface treatment of that wall, a CONSTRUCTION ELEVATION would tear away the surface and show the inner armature, bracing, materials, and techniques. Most of the time a REAR ELEVATION will reveal this information, but in the case of most three-dimensional scenery it will not.

There may be some instances where you will need to make a slight modification to an existing flat. For example you may need to hang a picture in a place on a wall which has no toggle behind it to attach the picture hanging hardware. To draft a REAR ELEVATION to show the position of the new toggle would probably take longer than cutting and attaching it. In situations such as these, it is best to indicate the position of the toggle in the FRONT ELEVATION with a dashed, hidden-construction line. All dashed lines in any scenic drafting must be identified with a note as to what they represent.

Other Sources of Information

DIMENSIONS—Not all of the information in an ELEVATION will be *drawn* on the scenery. Information such as dimensions for instance, will be *written out* next to the drawing. Every ELEVATION is to be fully dimensioned using the three layer system discussed in the previous section on dimensions. Occasionally a drawing is too big to fit on one sheet. In cases where the "middle" of the scenery is the same as the top and bottom it is acceptable to "tear out" this "middle" part of the drawing. This is called break-

ing the drawing. Special break lines are used to indicate where the break has been made.

BREAK LINE

In these cases you still need to indicate the full unbroken dimension on this compressed drawing. A special compressed dimension line is used to indicate this. Its strange appearance puts everyone reading the plans on notice that this particular dimension is not measurable with a scale rule.

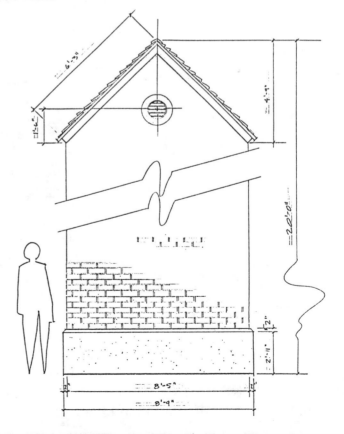

FIGURES—Human scale figures are helpful in comprehending the size of the scenery to be built. The perceived scale of a unit can be quite different from the size that it will actually be. A person drawn in your <u>ELEVATIONS</u> once in a while is an excellent way to keep the overall size of the scenery in proportion. (See page 76.)

LEADERS—You will communicate much of the information through notes which refer to and explain something that is drawn but may not be too clear. For instance you may have drawn a door knob but you need to identify the exact style or type. To make this identification you would write the information just outside the <u>ELEVATION</u> and draw an arrow pointing to it.

Information that needs to be repeated over and over in a drawing can be a problem. For instance you may have a drawing with lots of paneling that is outlined in 1×4 and routed with a particular bit. Rather than point to each board that needs to be routed, you can have a leader note that says ROUTED EDGES—BIT #12 TYP. The abbreviation for the word "typical" tips us off to the fact that you need this done in all cases. "Typical" notes need to be in the first (upper left) drawing in which they appear on a page. You can repeat them for emphasis if you like, but they must be seen right away.

LEADER LINE

This special note arrow and line is called a leader. Leader lines should not be exactly vertical or exactly horizontal. It's even a good idea to make them slightly curved. This is to keep the leader line from being confused with a dimension line or object outline. The leader is a light-weight line that ends in a half or filled in (closed) arrow actually touching the object that it is pointed to.

NOTE BOX—General information that pertains to the whole drawing or information regarding one or two drawings on the page that can't be expressed with a leader is placed in a note box.

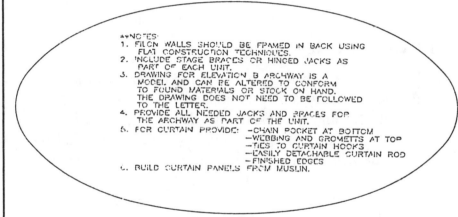

This box is placed somewhere on the sheet where it can easily be found, and is enclosed with its own border to make it stand out. The notes are numbered and are worded in the form of a command. For example, rather than "If it's not too much trouble, I think I want to cover the platforms with ⅛″ Masonite," the note should read..."SURFACE ALL PLATFORMS WITH ⅛″ MASO."

Here is a list of the type of information that would either be included in a note box or dealt with using leaders.

1. SUPPORT—What holds the scenery up? Common methods include stage braces, hinged or rigid jacks, tip jacks, rigged to fly, etc. In addition to the name of the method, you need to disclose any and all hardware needed

for the support and where it goes; stage brace cleats, hanging irons, etc.—fully dimensioned.

2. HARDWARE—Door knobs, hinges, latches, etc.—fully dimensioned.

3. MATERIALS—You must identify ALL construction materials; muslin flat, hardwall flat, 1×6 trim, Plexiglas in the windows, etc.

4. DETAILS—All details applied to the scenery must be identified. Plaster column capital, vacuum formed cornice molding, painted detail, plastic ivy, shake shingles, etc.

ELEVATION Key Markers

ELEVATIONS are drawn in the same order in which the scenery occurs onstage—downstage right to downstage left. First, the main set walls are drawn followed by the next "layer" of scenery—the backing flats, succeeded by walls even further upstage and then any drops, ground rows, etc. beyond. Each ELEVATION is "keyed" to the FLOOR PLAN with a special symbol. If this is done correctly it should be a simple matter for the carpenter using a particular ELEVATION to go back to the FLOOR PLAN and see how it fits in to the whole PLAN.

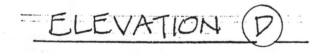

Each ELEVATION is titled and keyed like the previous example using ¼″ high letters. The letter D in the circle following the word ELEVATION is the identifier that you

assign. The scenery closest to D.S. right will be given the letter A and the scenery or drop furthest upstage and left will be given the highest letter. Double letters (AA) are used if you have more than 26 elevations. This same identification letter will be found on the PLAN. The first ELEVATION (the wall down right on the set) would be ELEVATION A so this ELEVATION D title refers to the fourth wall from downstage right.

The title is placed beneath the ELEVATION and below the last dimension line. Optional information that further describes the drawing could also be included such as HOSPITAL WALL S.R. If the scale for this particular ELEVATION was different from the scale in the title block it must be indicated below in the ELEVATION title.

This marker appears on the FLOOR PLAN pointing directly at the wall or scenic element that you have drawn the ELEVATION of. The base of the arrow should be parallel to the plane in which the ELEVATION is drawn. Notice the very particular shape of the marker. Try to avoid making up your own version of this symbol. This symbol is standard on all professional drawings. Also avoid putting this symbol on your ELEVATIONS. Both of these are common mistakes that many beginners make. The ELEVATION marker key has just the circle—no arrow.

Layout

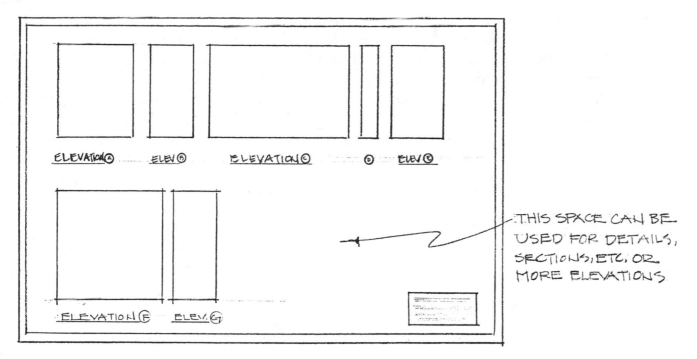

ELEVATION Ⓐ .... ELEV Ⓑ   ELEVATION ⒸC .... ⒹD ELEV ⒺE

THIS SPACE CAN BE
USED FOR DETAILS,
SECTIONS, ETC. OR
MORE ELEVATIONS

ELEVATION ⒻF   ELEV. ⒼG

A sheet of ELEVATIONS is typically laid out with all ELE-VATIONS sharing a common baseline and going from the upper left to the upper right across the page. If there is room, another row is drawn below the first. If there is still more room another row is drawn. The upper left most ELEVATION on this sheet (not on the PLAN) has the lowest letter on the sheet and the lower right ELEVATION on this sheet (not on the PLAN) has the highest letter. This will continue on for several sheets. Mixed in with these ELEVATIONS will be DETAIL drawings, REAR ELEVA-TIONS, SECTIONS, etc.

If the set is complicated it is a good idea (not required)

to put a ½″ scale PLAN view of the walls drafted on this sheet in the lower left-hand corner of the sheet. This is particularly important in cases such as a wagon set in a musical. Perhaps all of the ELEVATIONS for that set are on one sheet of drafting. A ½″ scale plan here on the same sheet helps everyone understand orientation of all of the walls to each other.

All ELEVATIONS fall into two categories. ELEVATION is really the *last* name for both categories. They also have a first name which describes them in a bit more detail—PROJECTED and EXTENDED. Revealing this first name can be crucial to how the drawing is interpreted.

PROJECTED ELEVATIONS

The types of ELEVATIONS we have discussed so far happen to be PROJECTED elevations. Most ELEVATIONS are are indeed PROJECTED ELEVATIONS. (PROJECTED ELEVATIONS rarely use their first name.) When we defined ELEVATIONS as "...a straight on, flattened out, full face no perspective view of that part of the set..." we were describing PROJECTED ELEVATIONS.

If the scenery on the PLAN is NOT parallel to the base of the elevation marker and is instead at an angle to it, then the ELEVATION drawing of that scenery will result in a foreshortened wall. This of course can be quite confusing and we avoid it most of the time by having an ELEVATION for each plane, or change of direction of each wall.

PROJECTED ELEVATIONS with foreshortened elements are sometimes used when the wall is quite typical and it saves time, space, or both to combine it with another ELEVATION and draw it this way. If the wall or scenery does have foreshortening in it which might lead to error or confusion when it is built (due to the fact that its apparent width doesn't match its measured width), then it must be labeled with its "first name," PROJECTED ELEVATION.

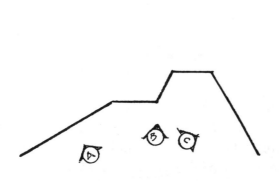

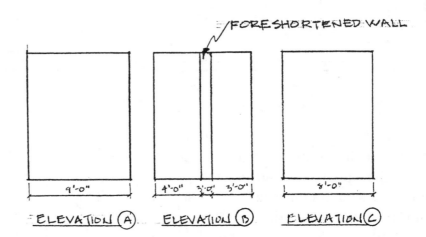

EXTENDED ELEVATIONS

EXTENDED ELEVATIONS take walls that are combined in an elevation marker (as those in ELEVATION B were in the previous example) and instead of foreshortening them, "pulls them out flat" or *extends* them in the ELEVATIONS. This is done despite their planar relationship in the PLAN. This too can lead to confusion. To avoid mixups, EXTENDED ELEVATIONS are *always* labeled as EXTENDED ELEVATIONS.

The drawing below takes the same FLOOR PLAN we used in the PROJECTED ELEVATIONS example and uses the exact same elevation marker configuration. The results are a very different set of ELEVATIONS. As you draft you will discover that there are times when an angled piece of scenery is adequately represented in a PROJECTED ELEVATION, but when that view is not adequate an EXTENDED ELEVATION may be the solution to your drafting problems. A big advantage that the EXTENDED ELEVATION (in this example) has over three separate ELEVATIONS is the time that can be saved in labeling and dimensioning (if the three walls are quite similar).

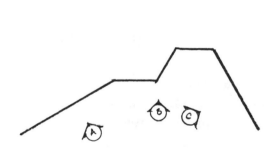

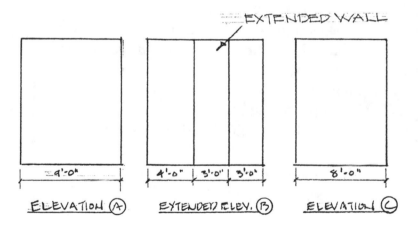

EXTENDED WALL

ELEVATION Ⓐ   EXTENDED ELEV. Ⓑ   ELEVATION Ⓒ

Checklist

Use this checklist to be sure that you are including the necessary information in your <u>ELEVATIONS</u>.

☐ ¾″ border drawn around the sheet

☐ Walls or units drawn in medium-weight line

☐ All detail required for construction drawn

☐ If needed, additional views are drawn of each piece of scenery:

   —<u>SIDE ELEVATIONS</u>
   —<u>REAR ELEVATIONS</u>
   —<u>CONSTRUCTION ELEVATIONS</u>
   —<u>SECTION VIEWS</u>
   —<u>DETAIL DRAWINGS</u>

☐ All painted or applied detail is drawn on the unit and dimensioned

☐ Each drawing is fully dimensioned

☐ Any special construction techniques are noted or drawn

☐ Information about how the scenery is supported is complete

☐ Information about all hardware and rigging is complete

☐ <u>ELEVATIONS</u> properly titled and coded

☐ Title block drawn in lower right hand corner

Project 7   <u>ELEVATIONS</u>

1. Draw a border.
2. Lay out your title block.
3. Draft a set of <u>ELEVATIONS</u> for the ¼″ <u>FLOOR PLAN</u> below.
4. Draft a <u>REAR ELEVATION</u> of the door flat.
5. Finish your title block.

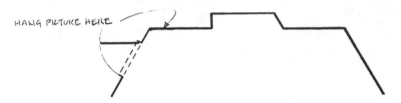

HANG PICTURE HERE

SPECIFICATIONS

a. All walls are 14′ tall.

b. The door is 7′ tall.

c. All walls have a 6″ base board.

d. Draw a 4″ trim around the door.

e. The picture is to be hung so that the top of it is 8′ from the floor.

f. There is a 3″ chair rail all around the set.

g. The door flat must be put on caster jacks.

h. The stage left wall must fly away in the third act.

i. Research and use Victorian period detail in the <u>ELEVATIONS</u>.

j. Wall widths from D.R. to D.L. are 6′-0″, 5′-0″, 1′-0″, 5′-0″, 1′-0″, 5′-0″, 6′-0″.

k. Door is 2′-6″ wide.

9. Sections

To adequately explain intricate scenic elements or three dimensional scenery in your drafting, you will need to augment the ELEVATIONS with more illustrative or revealing drawings. One such drawing is the SECTION view. A SECTION view is a drawing of the set piece as if it has been cut all the way through a "telling" portion. The front part is then removed. This "sliced through" view can reveal much about the hidden infrastructure and/or the profile or depth of the object. There are two types of SECTION drawings—the REMOVED SECTION and the REVOLVED SECTION. Each shows the same view but each is placed in a different proximity to the drawing.

REMOVED SECTION

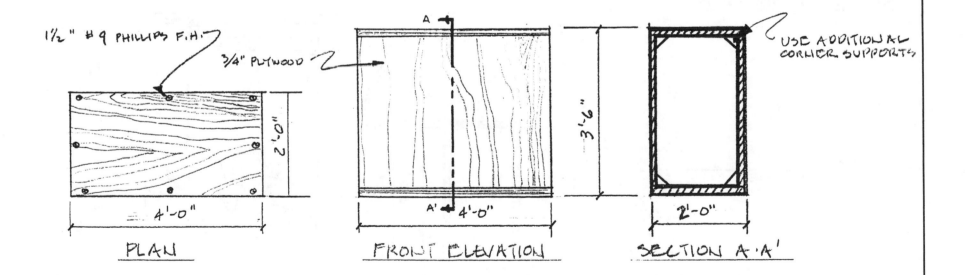

The example above is of a simple box made of plywood. Although a SIDE ELEVATION has not been provided, it too would show you a slab of plywood. The inner structure of the box would still have been hidden from view. Only a SECTION can reveal the construction in the interior. To the right of the ELEVATION view above is the REMOVED SECTION. After the imaginary slice was made, it was *removed*, turned 90°, and then drawn next to the ELEVATION. Now we can see that the box is to be made hollow with 45° angle corner supports placed at each joint. Heavy-weight (extra thick) lines are used for the parts of the drawing that the imaginary saw blade touched. This is why heavy-weight lines are often called section lines.

In order to orient the viewer correctly as to how the SECTION view relates to the original drawing, a special line is drawn on the original drawing, at the plane of the imaginary slice.

This line is called a cutting plane line. An example of it can be found on the FRONT ELEVATION of the box. It is a medium-weight (thick) line broken with paired dashes. A longer cutting plane line would have only one set. Two arrows on the ends show the person reading the plans the direction orientation of the REMOVED SECTION. The tip of each arrow is then labeled with a letter, one of which has a prime (′) after it reserved for the bottom or right side arrow. The SECTION view is then labeled accordingly. In this illustration it is labeled SECTION A A′.

REVOLVED SECTION

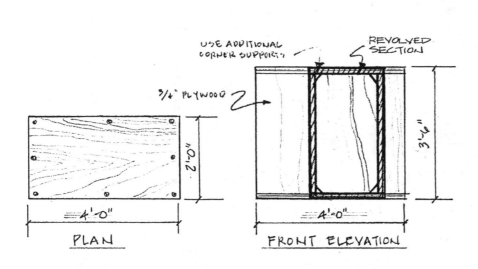

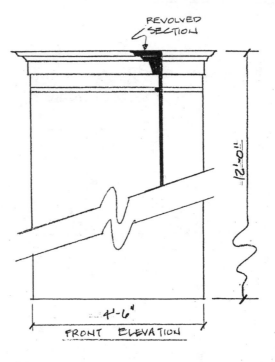

The REVOLVED SECTION is also a sliced through view of an object which has been *revolved* 90°. Its purpose is identical to that of the REMOVED SECTION—to reveal information about the interior construction or profile depth of an object. The difference is that the REVOLVED SECTION is placed directly on the ELEVATION from which it is derived. Since a complicated SECTION drawn on an ELEVATION could become quite confusing, this drawing is usually reserved for more basic tasks. Rather than being used to reveal complex construction techniques, the REVOLVED SECTION is better suited to quickly show the depth of 3-D details on a unit which otherwise appears flat in the ELEVATION. A very common use of the REVOLVED SECTION is to illustrate molding profile depth such as that of the cornice, chair rail, and base board.

Horizontally oriented REVOLVED SECTIONS appearing on ELEVATIONS are called REVOLVED PLANS. They perform the same function as the REVOLVED SECTION but this orientation forces them to be called simply PLAN views superimposed on the ELEVATIONS. They are an invaluable tool to reflect jogs, reveals, and other changes of direction in otherwise deceptively flat looking ELEVATIONS. You can see examples of this in some of the drawings provided in the section on ELEVATIONS.

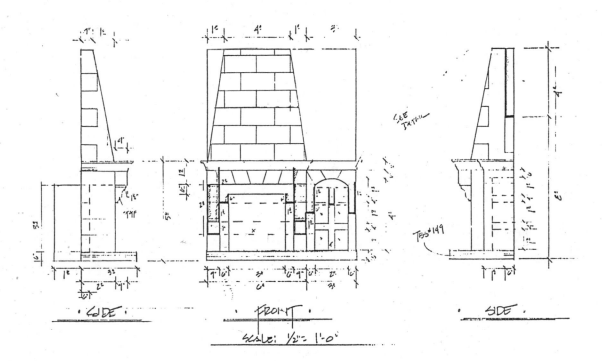

Murphy Brown (Television) fireplace DETAIL using REVOLVED PLANS and SECTIONS.

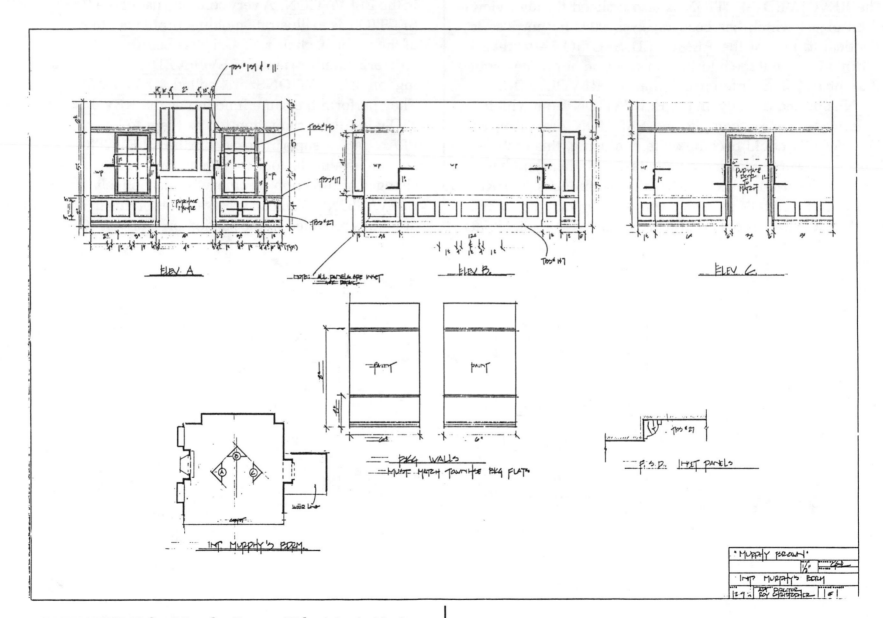

<u>ELEVATIONS</u> for *Murphy Brown* (Television). Notice
the extensive use of <u>REVOLVED PLANS</u>.

Project 8   SECTIONS

1. Draw a border.

2. Lay out your title block.

3. Obtain a three-dimensional scenic element (fireplace mantel unit, cornice molding, small prop, etc.).

4. "Spec" the unit provided. That is, with note pad (or the space below), tape measure and pencil (no scale rule and no straight edge), draw several views of the object—complete with dimensions. An example of such a sketch (a fireplace unit) is provided on the next page.

5. On this one sheet of vellum, draft a FRONT ELEVA-TION, REMOVED SECTION, and REVOLVED PLAN.

6. Depending on the size of the object you choose, you may need to draw the object at a larger scale than ½". Re-member, DETAILS of small objects are often drawn in a larger scale so that they can provide as much information as accurately as possible.

7. Finish your title block.

This project will not only give you experience in draw-ing SECTIONS but will also give you a chance to sketch an existing object in order to prepare it to be included in a new production. Normally if the unit is stock, you would not draw it with the amount of detail with which you will be drawing this object. In that situation you might simply out-line the space that the object takes up and leave the interior of that space completely blank except to identify the unit. Inside the space you would write STOCK FIREPLACE UNIT #57.

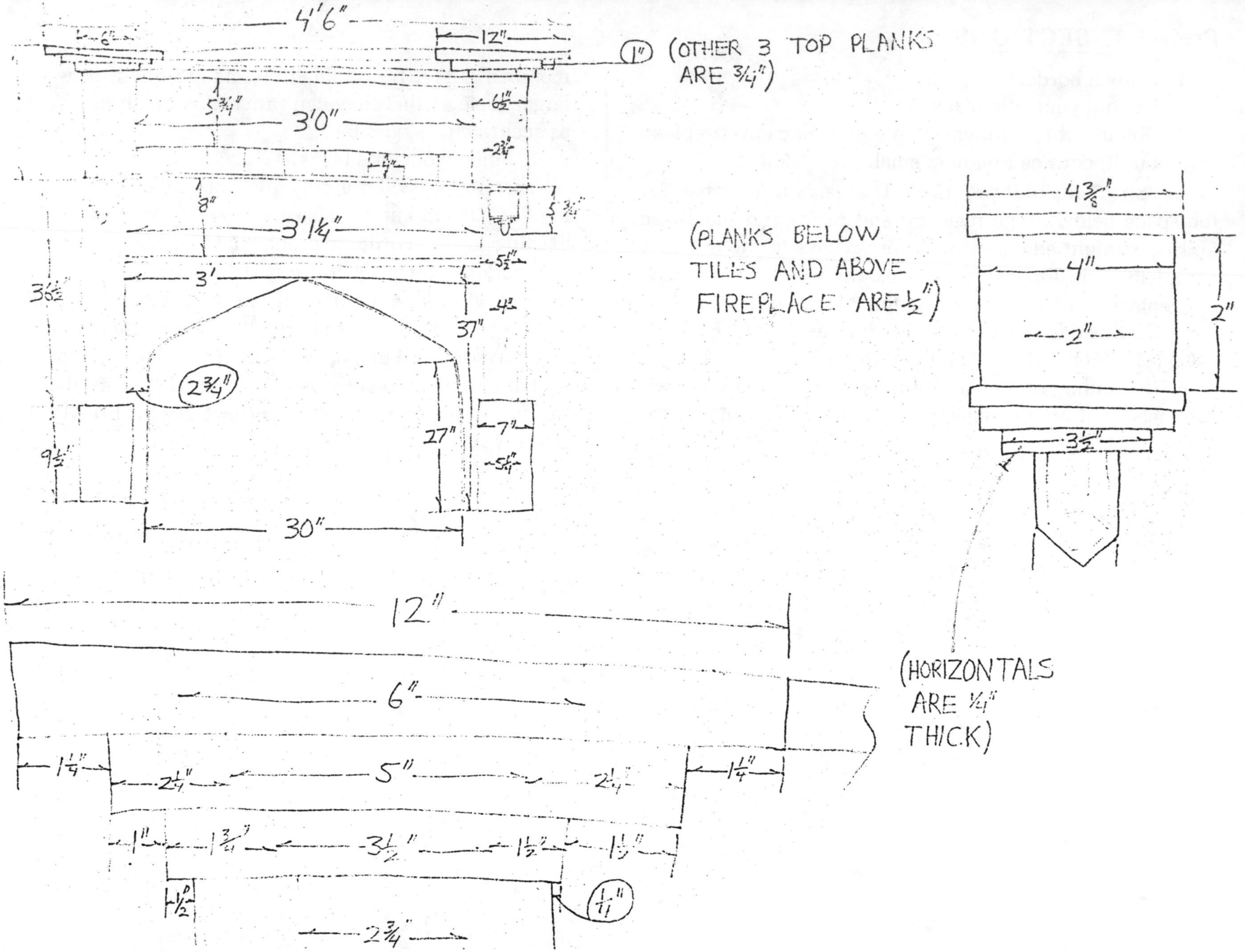

4'6"

6" 12"

1" (OTHER 3 TOP PLANKS
ARE ¾")

5¾" 3'0" 6½"

2¾"

4"

8" 3'1¼" 5¾"

3'0" 3' 5½"

36½" 37" 4"

2¾"

27" 7"

9½" 5¼"

30"

(PLANKS BELOW
TILES AND ABOVE
FIREPLACE ARE ½")

4⅜"

4"

2" 2"

3½"

12"

6"

(HORIZONTALS
ARE ¼"
THICK)

1¼" 2¼" 5" 2¼" 1¼"

1" 1¾" 3½" 1½" 1½"

1½"

1¼"

2¾"

10. Details

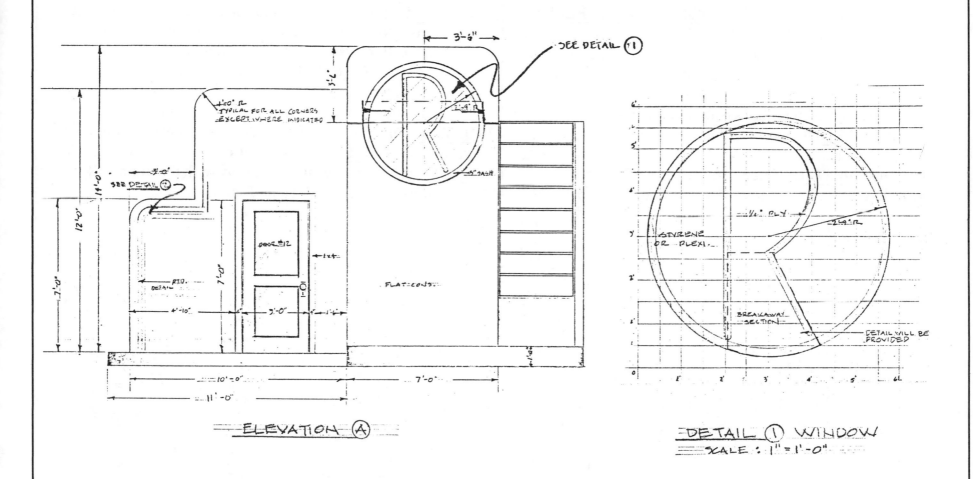

ELEVATION (A)

DETAIL ① WINDOW
SCALE : 1" = 1'-0"

If the <u>ELEVATION</u> you have just drawn doesn't quite tell enough about construction, techniques, and materials, you need to augment it with more drawings. If after having drawn <u>REAR ELEVATIONS</u>, <u>REMOVED SECTIONS</u>, and <u>CONSTRUCTION ELEVATIONS</u> you find that you're still not able to get across enough information about particular parts of the drawing, then you probably need to draft <u>DETAILS</u>.

A <u>DETAIL</u> drawing is no more than a specific part of of the scenic unit redrawn at a larger scale. It is primarily used when a large amount of information needs to be told about a small part of the set and there just isn't room enough to do so in the <u>ELEVATION</u> (or <u>REAR ELEVATION</u>, or <u>PLAN</u>, or <u>REMOVED SECTION</u>, etc.)

This drawing should be placed as close as possible to the drawing from which it originates. A second choice would be to locate it somewhere else on that same sheet. <u>DETAILS</u> are even sometimes gathered together and drawn on separate <u>DETAIL</u> sheets that are found at the end of the set of blueprints.

Because <u>DETAILS</u> often stray from their drawing of origin, they must be carefully labeled and referred to. In the example above you see the reference SEE <u>DETAIL</u> #1 connected to the drawing with a leader. The drawing itself is then labeled <u>DETAIL</u> #1 WINDOW. <u>DETAILS</u> are always numbered beginning with #1 at the beginning of the plans and ending with the highest number at the back of the plans. Numbers do not repeat for each page of the drafting. Letters are never used for details. Letter designations are reserved for <u>ELEVATIONS</u> and <u>SECTIONS</u> only.

Since the scale of <u>DETAIL</u> drawing is so variable, it is very important to include it below the title. Many times <u>DETAILS</u> are drawn to full scale. This is always the case with <u>REMOVED SECTION</u> views of moldings. A full scale <u>DETAIL</u> is commonly written simply with the initials F.S.D. The letters stand for Full Scale Detail.

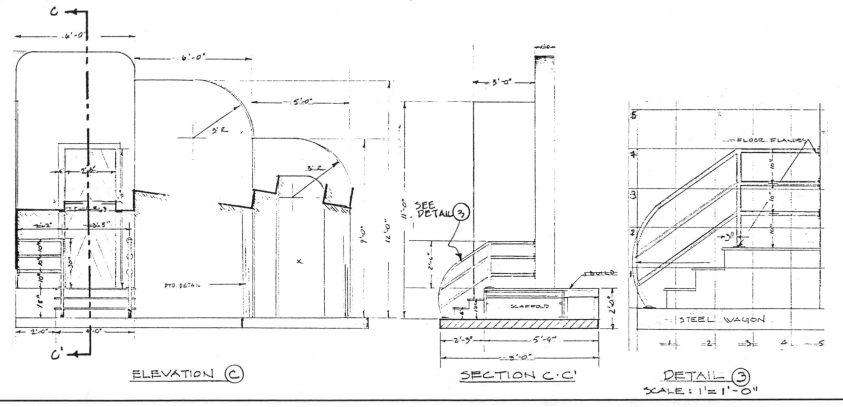

ELEVATION C   SECTION C·C'   DETAIL 3
                                           SCALE: 1" = 1'-0"

In the example above, the draftsperson decided to make another drawing in order to show both the step unit construction and to reveal the railing design. The <u>ELEVATION</u> view was not effective in exhibiting either of these features, forcing the development of <u>DETAIL</u>—in this case a <u>REMOVED SECTION</u>. However, in order to describe the railing configuration even better, it was decided to draw a 1″ <u>DETAIL</u> of it. Because of the irregular shape of the curved railing, radii could not be used to explain the shape and size. Instead a grid was used. This gridded pattern

was enlarged by the shop to full scale, and then the pipe for the handrail was bent right on top of this modified outline (sometimes called a template). This very same pattern, drawn on plywood, was used beneath the pipe that was cut, bent, and welded together to fabricate the complete deco handrail. The <u>DETAIL</u> on this sheet shows <u>DETAIL #2</u> from the same <u>ELEVATION</u>. This <u>DETAIL</u> was originally drawn full scale but has been reduced to fit it on these pages. <u>DETAIL #2</u> shows the radii of art deco stripes as they round a corner of the set.

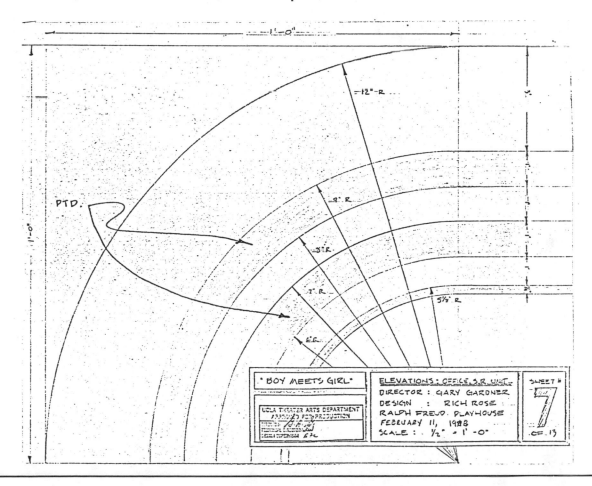

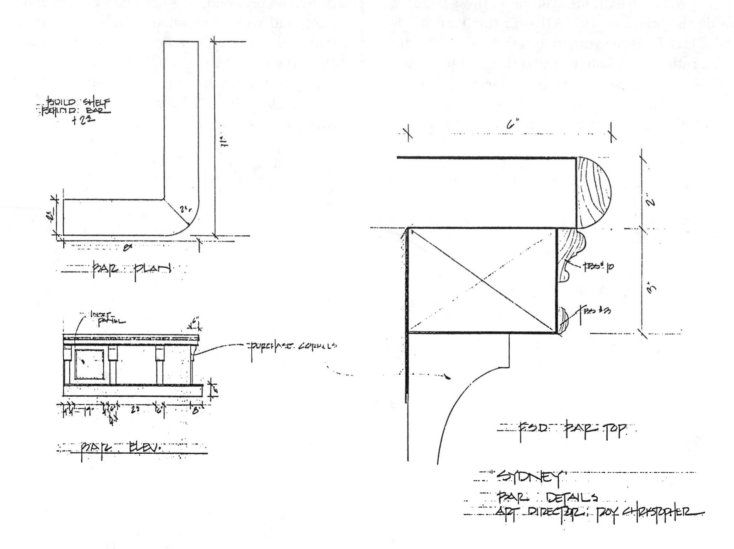

BUILD SHELF
BEHIND BAR
+2"

7'-1"

4"

2"r

8"

BAR PLAN

INSET
PANEL

PURCHASE CORNICE

BAR ELEV.

6"

2"

FSD'D TRIM

3"

FSD #3

FSD BAR TOP

"SYDNEY"
BAR DETAILS
ART DIRECTOR: ROY CHRISTOPHER

Full scale molding <u>DETAIL</u> (REMOVED SECTION).

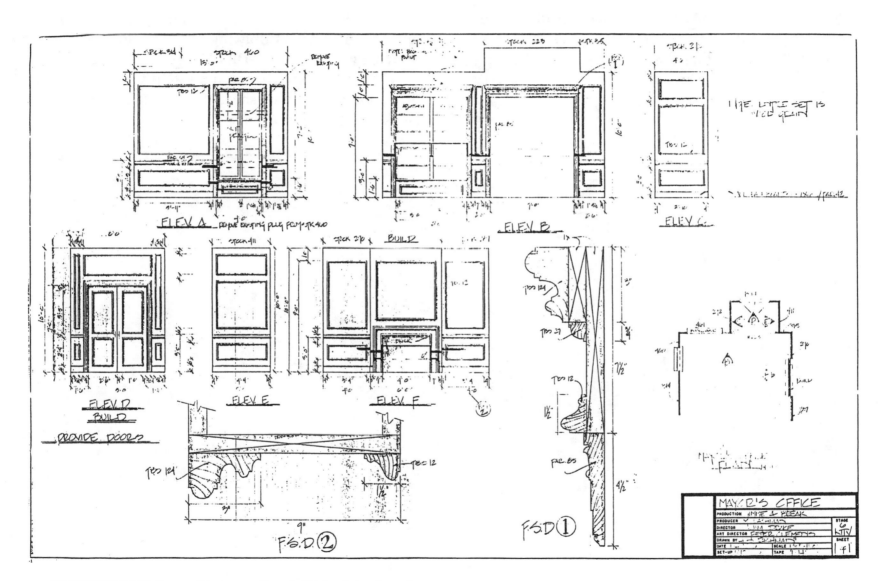

ELEVATIONS from *Gimme a Break* (Television) making extensive use of <u>REMOVED SECTIONS</u> and <u>REVOLVED PLANS</u>.

Project 9   DETAILS

1. Draw a full scale <u>DETAIL</u> of some part of the unit you drew in the previous project.

2. The <u>DETAIL</u> could be either a larger scale drawing of a small intricate part of the unit, or a full scale <u>DETAIL</u> of a portion of the object.

3. Refer to this <u>DETAIL</u> and number it with a leader note on the original drawing. Be sure to label this new drawing with that same <u>DETAIL</u> #.

4. Place this drawing on the PROJECT 8 sheet if it will fit. If not, begin a new sheet. Be sure to include your title block and a border.

11. Center Line Vertical Section

A crucial tool of the theatrical scenic designer as well as the lighting designer is the CENTER LINE VERTICAL SECTION. "The SECTION," as it is most often referred to, is a vertical dissected view of the entire theater that includes the audience seating. The cutting plane for this view is the center line. The "cut" goes through all scenery on the deck and all scenery that is flown, including masking. It also shows the positions of all ante-proscenium, as well as onstage, electrics.

While the SECTION is being developed it should go through three important phases.

SCENIC DESIGNER PHASE—In this phase the scenic designer uses the section to determine:

—how tall teasers (borders) can be

—where the borders should be to mask the theater, top of the cyc, scrims and drops, and any flown scenery

—how tall flown scenery can be and remain out of sight lines

—where any flown scenery can be

—if upper levels of the set are visible to high or balcony rows of the audience

—the the height that the ground rows need to be

—where any ground rows need to be

—the desired amount of visual space above the set (how much cyc or black above the set itself should be seen)

LIGHTING DESIGNER PHASE—The lighting designer then takes the SECTION, as it is currently configured, and begins to do his or her calculations. The CENTER LINE VERTICAL SECTION is used by the lighting designer to determine:

—lighting angles and optimum instrument position

—where additional masking needs to be, in order to mask lighting instruments

At this point the lighting designer takes note of where some of the optimum lighting positions conflict with scenery or masking placed by the scenic designer.

COLLABORATION PHASE—The scenic and lighting designer then get together to solve the conflicts that the lighting designer has noted earlier. Often it is a simple matter for the scenic designer to move some of the flown scenery to another counterweight pipe or raise or lower, add or take away a border. It is in the scenic designer's interest to accommodate the lighting designer to the full extent possible. After all, if the lighting designer is hindered and the lighting is bad, then the set will look bad too. Sometimes such compromises on the scenic designer's part are not possible. There may not be another place for that flying unit. Or perhaps a border can't be raised because doing so will expose the grid. In these instances the lighting designer must be flexible and have other solutions to fall back on.

Collaborations such as these are always the ideal but are not always possible. The lighting designer may be in Chicago and the set designer in Atlanta, making a meeting on the SECTION difficult to arrange. Every effort for face-to-face collaboration should be made, but some alternatives do exist. Overnight mail is an excellent second best method of communication. Many designers are blueprinting drawings, cutting them up and "faxing" them back and forth. If you don't have a fax machine there is likely to be a store nearby that will send and receive fax communications. This might be a store which specializes in fax or it might be your corner instant printing place or drug store.

In the instances where designers can't collaborate it's a good idea for the set designer to go through the "three phases" of collaboration anyway. The set designer should extend the courtesy of putting him or herself in the shoes of the lighting designer by taking the issues involved with lighting the set into account while drafting the <u>SECTION</u>.

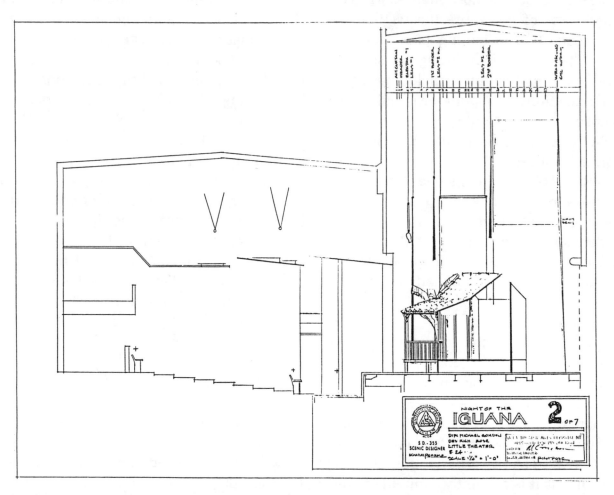

<u>CL</u> <u>SECTION</u> for *Night of the Iguana* (Theater).

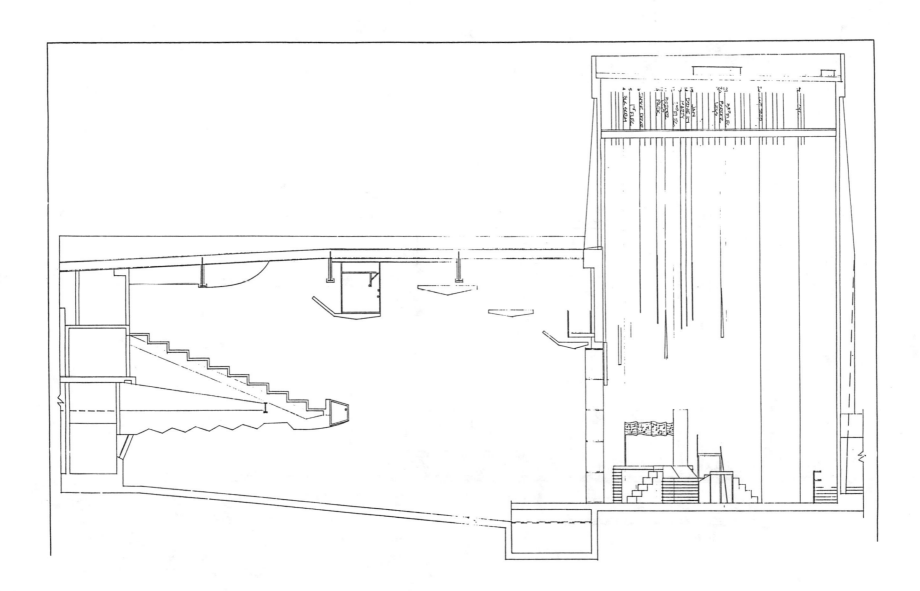

<u>CL SECTION</u> for *Grease* (Theater).

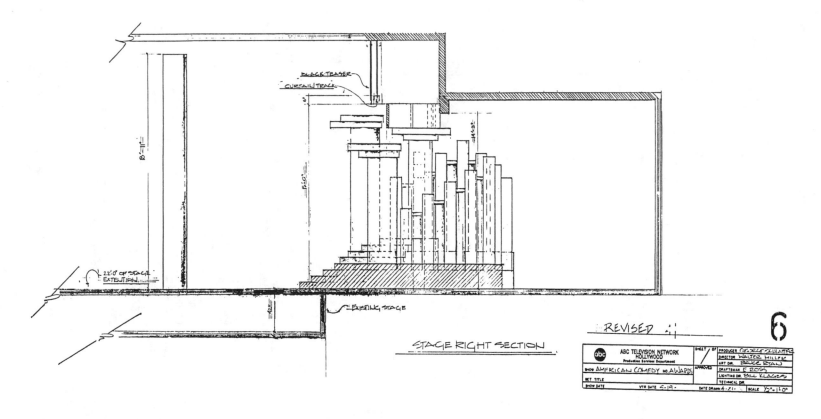

STAGE RIGHT SECTION

REVISED

6

	ABC TELEVISION NETWORK HOLLYWOOD Production Services Department	SHEET 1 OF	PRODUCER GEORGE SCHLATTER
			DIRECTOR WALTER MILLER
			ART DIR. BRUCE RYAN
	SHOW AMERICAN COMEDY no. AWARDS	APPROVED	DRAFTSMAN F. ROSS
	SET TITLE		LIGHTING DIR. BILL KLAGES
			TECHNICAL DIR.
	SHOW DATE	VTR DATE 5-19-	DATE DRAWN 4-21-	SCALE ½"=1'0"

CL SECTION for American Comedy Awards
(Television).

Developing a CENTER LINE VERTICAL SECTION

1. Tape a <u>CENTER LINE SECTION</u> of the performance space to your drafting table. Be careful to line up the vertical and horizontal lines of the drawing with your drafting machine.

2. Place a sheet of vellum over the blueprint.

3. Draw in the two critical sightlines.

The two critical sightlines are layout weight lines which begin at the seats closest to and furthest away from the stage. They intersect with the lowest point of the first masking piece (teaser, border, proscenium, or header) and continue on until they reach either the back wall or grid of the theater. We'll call them the first row critical sightline and the last row critical sightline.

4. Draw the sct on the stage (use layout weight line).

Drawing the set on the stage is a complex process that must be done with great precision. The concept of cutting the design in half and drafting it on the <u>SECTION</u> is illustrated in the example on the next page. Here are some guidelines to make the job easier:

a. Fold a copy of the <u>FLOOR PLAN</u> in half along the center line.

b. If your "blank" <u>SECTION</u> is of stage right, place the folded <u>PLAN</u> beneath your vellum with the stage right side up. (Reverse this if your "blank" is of stage left).

c. Line up your plan vertically and horizontally:

—Line up the center line of the <u>PLAN</u> with the long horizontal stage floor line of the <u>SECTION</u>.

—Find the edge of the stage on the <u>PLAN</u> and line it up with the edge of the stage on the <u>SECTION</u>.

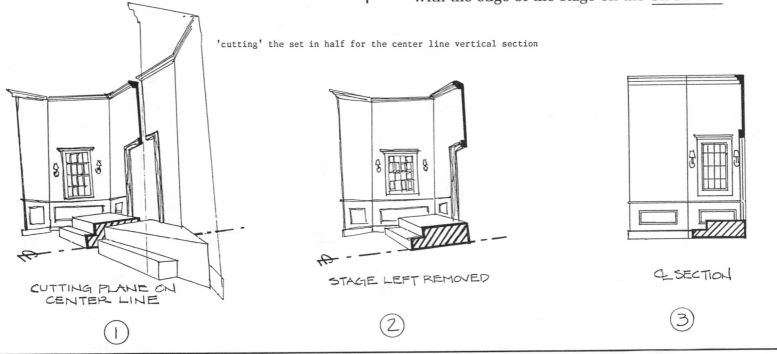

'cutting' the set in half for the center line vertical section

CUTTING PLANE ON CENTER LINE ①   STAGE LEFT REMOVED ②   CL SECTION ③

SECTION 2

d. Carefully tape down the folded <u>PLAN</u>.

e. Draw in the scenery.

—For each scenic unit or wall, draw a vertical line going up from the stage floor at the downstage and upstage edges.

—When this is complete, draw a line parallel to the <u>SECTION</u> stage floor that represents the height of the scenery.

—Fill in with the appropriate detail; doors, windows, fireplaces, etc.

—Once the set portion of the <u>SECTION</u> is complete, go back and use medium-weight lines for the outlines and heavy-weight lines for the sectioned or "cut" parts of the set.

f. The <u>SECTION</u> shows only half of the stage and therefore only half of the set. Scenery on the other part of the stage that is very different or critical for purposes of lighting or masking should be drawn in using a dashed line. To do this you will need to flip your <u>FLOOR PLAN</u> over, fold it in half along the center line, and tape it below the stage floor of the <u>SECTION</u> (reverse the process for a stage left <u>SECTION</u>).

g. Draw in all flown scenery, legs (tormentors), cyc, scrims, drops, etc.

5. Draw in the borders using heavy-weight (extra thick) lines. As a first rule of thumb, place the borders as far apart as possible. This will cause you to use the fewest number possible. The less cloth there is hanging above the stage to catch light, the better the stage picture will look. As a second rule of thumb, the bottom of the borders should line up along the back row critical sight line. This ensures that all of the audience sees roughly the same view of the stage. Place them higher if possible but never lower unless absolutely necessary. Placing them too high, however, can make the lighting designer's job quite difficult.

Let's draw the first border. You already know that the bottom of this first border needs to touch the last row critical sightline seat.

—Put a piece of tape on a vertical edge of your triangle starting at the bottom of the triangle. Measure up in scale the height of your border and make a mark on the tape. If your border is 15′ high then you would measure 15′ up from the bottom of your triangle and make a mark. We'll call this the upper limit mark.

—Place your triangle on your horizontal drafting arm (or parallel or T-square).

—Slowly and carefully slide your triangle along the drafting arm toward the back wall of the theater. As you do so keep the bottom left corner of the triangle right on top of the *last row critical sightline.* Keep your eye on the *first row critical sightline.*

—When your upper border limit mark gets within a foot of the *first row critical sightline* STOP! This is where the first border should go.

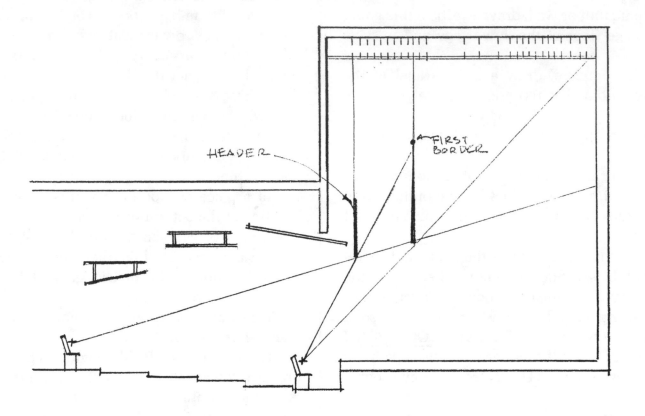

HEADER

FIRST BORDER

—Follow your triangle up to the counterweight line sets. If there is no line set that lines up with your triangle, or it is already reserved for something else, then put this first border on the closest downstage line set available. Never go upstage of a sightline to place your border.

—Place a mark on your <u>SECTION</u> at the bottom of the triangle and another at the upper border limit mark. Draw in your border. Borders are usually drawn as tall skinny triangles. The triangle represents the fullness of the border. Borders that are weighted with a pipe and therefore have no fullness should be drawn simply as a heavy-weight line. Don't forget to draw a line from the top of the pipe to the counterweight line set in the grid.

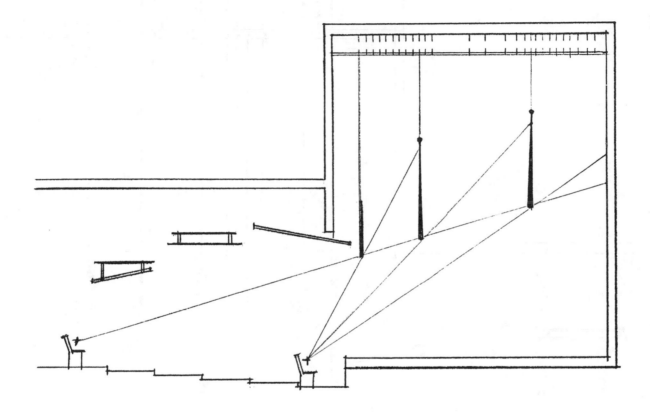

—After you have drawn the first border you need to draw an adjusted sightline from the first row seat which intersects with the bottom of the first border and continues on until it hits the back wall of the theater or the grid. After each border is drawn you draw a new adjusted sightline from the first row. Only then can you draw a third and any subsequent borders. The position of each border should be determined by:

—The rules outlined above.

—The first row critical or adjusted sightline hitting just below the top of each border.

—The need to mask the top of the cyc, scrims, drops, etc.

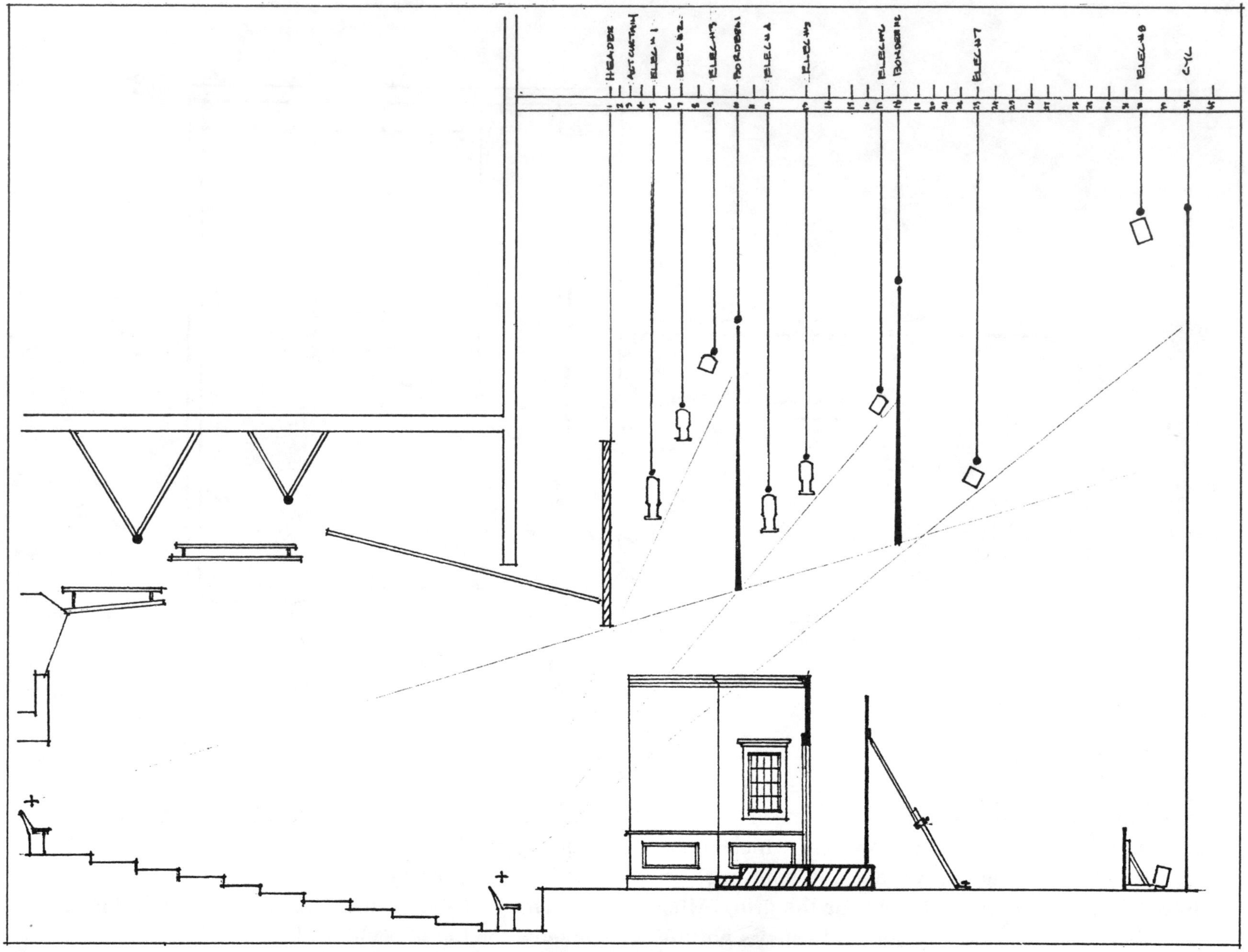
HEADER
ACT CURTAIN
ELEC #1
ELEC #2
ELEC #3
BORDER #1
ELEC #4
ELEC #5
ELEC #6
BORDER #2
ELEC #7
ELEC #8
CYC

—The need to mask any flown scenery.

—The need to mask lighting instruments.

6. Label what is on each line set.

7. Analyze the position of the set on the stage. Make sure that the audience sees all that it is supposed to see and nothing else.

8. If there are any floor electrics, make sure that they are masked properly, especially from the balcony seats.

9. Check the balcony or last row sightline to see if any porch tops, roofs, etc. can be seen. If so, take a note to specify any detail or painting that will need to be done.

10. Draw in the theater architecture in medium-weight line.

11. Draw in your title block.

12. Schedule a meeting with the lighting designer to begin the second phase of the SECTION's development.

Checklist

Use this checklist to be sure that you are including the necessary information in your CENTER LINE VERTICAL SECTION.

☐ ¾″ border
☐ Theater architecture drawn including
  —Locking or pin rail
  —Critical sightline seats and sightlines
  —Catwalks
  —Grid
  —Permanent lighting positions
☐ Set drawn on stage
☐ All vertical masking (legs) drawn
☐ All overhead electrics drawn (following the collaboration with the lighting designer)
☐ All flown scenery drawn
☐ All floor lighting equipment drawn and masked (following the collaboration with the lighting designer)
☐ Every sightline has been checked from the first row sightline seat past the bottom of each border to make sure that each adjusted sightline hits just below the top of another border (except for the last sightline which may hit just below the top of the cyc or a drop, etc.)
☐ All electrics are out of sightlines
☐ All flown scenery can be hidden out of sightlines
☐ Tops of cycs, scrims, drops, etc. are masked
☐ Title block drawn in

12. Organizing the Plans

The working drawings are traditionally organized in a distinctive order for maximum clarity.

All drawings should be drawn in ½″ scale if possible (except for DETAILS). The PLAN and SECTION may need to be done in ¼″ scale if the sheet size becomes too large for one reason or another. Each drawing should remain consistent; each should have the same sheet size (usually 24″×36″) and the same border and title block design. Each sheet should be numbered consecutively.

Here is a list of all of the drawings that make up a complete set of working drawings. They are listed in the order that they should occur.

1. PERSPECTIVE SKETCH(ES) OF THE SCENERY—Blueprinted sketches are optional but are quite helpful to the shop. They provide the carpenter building the set a quick way to reference how any particular piece of scenery being built fits into the whole scheme of things. Although a model and/or rendering may have been provided, a sketch attached to the plan is very handy. Perspective scenery sketches are covered later in SECTION 16.

2. FLOOR PLAN(S)/STAGING PLAN(S)—The PLAN is the next (or first) sheet in the drawings. You may have to draw several PLANS if it is a multi-set production. You can save drawing time with multiple PLANS by using a brown-line or photocopy technique (described on the next page).

3. CENTER LINE VERTICAL SECTION(S)—If each side of the stage is very different it may be necessary to draw a SECTION for each half.

4. PLATFORM PLAN(S)—Often the PLATFORM PLAN will not fit on one sheet. You may need to "break" it and draw it on two or more sheets.

5. ELEVATIONS—Each sheet may contain:
—FRONT ELEVATIONS
—REAR ELEVATIONS
—CONSTRUCTION DRAWINGS
—REVOLVED SECTION
—REMOVED SECTIONS
—DETAIL DRAWINGS

6. DETAIL DRAWINGS—If not included on the ELEVATION sheets, these drawings would appear together on one or several sheets at the end of the set of working drawings.

Brown-Line (or Photocopy) Technique

This technique is designed to save the time spent in drawing the common elements of the FLOOR PLANS of multi-set shows. The brown-line method uses the blueprint machine process with a special brown-line paper. This paper is as translucent as vellum and will blueprint nicely. You can even erase parts of the brown-lined copy with a special correction fluid available at blueprint copy and supply stores.

1. The first step in both of these processes is to draw all of the "basic" set, stage, masking, audience area, etc. that is consistent with each PLAN, on a sheet of vellum.

2. You then make a brown-line (sometimes called "sepia") or photocopy for each different FLOOR PLAN arrangement.

3. The next step is to draw each particular set configuration on each of the brown-line or photocopies.

Warning! Pencil line mistakes can be erased on the sepia but the erasures show up highly accentuated on the blueprint (big white blobs). It might be better to make extra sepias and start over if you make a major mistake rather than erasing.

4. Next, you either photocopy the photocopy or blueprint the brown-line of each of these unique PLANS.

It might sound a little complex but it really isn't. It will save you valuable hours of drafting time. You can even use this technique for your sketches. You might have a basic set drawn on vellum and then make several photocopies or brown-lines. On each copy you can draw on the scenery that flies or moves on for each scene. This technique may even have uses for you in drawing ELEVATIONS and developing REAR ELEVATIONS. Once it has been photocopied or blueprinted it's genuinely difficult to detect that you've "cheated."

The End of the Beginning

This marks the halfway point of *Drafting Scenery*. In this first half we have covered all the basic drawings and techniques involved in drafting a complete set of working drawings. This next project (PROJECT 10) will give you the chance to put your newly acquired skills into practice. You will be quite surprised to learn that your hard work is paying off. You will soon find out that you have learned quite a lot about drafting a complete scenic design.

With this second half of the book you will build on this base in order to develop new techniques that will permit you to enrich your working drawings even more.

Project 10   A Complete Set of Working Drawings

1. Draft a complete set of working drawings for the set described in the sketch and FLOOR PLAN provided on the next two pages. Notice that this set is drawn in no particular historical period. Research a historical architectural period such as Georgian. Incorporate your research into the architectural details of this set.

2. Draw a complete set of furniture on the PLAN.

3. Draw all masking on the FLOOR PLAN and SECTION. Include a non-wraparound cyc.

4. Add landscaping (trees, bushes, etc.) outside the windows.

5. The scale of the project PLAN provided is ¼" = 1'-0". Put only layout dimensions on your FLOOR PLAN. The dimensions provided are for information only.

6. Use the checklists presented in the previous sections of the book to make sure you are including all of the necessary information.

7. SPECIFICATIONS:
—Wall height = 12'-0"
—Height of bookcase, window, arch opening = 9'-6"
—Fireplace mantel height = 5'-0"
—Fireplace opening height = 3'-0"
—Wainscot height = 3'-0"
—Window seat height = 1'-6"
—Step height = 6"
—Bookcase bottom shelf = 2'-0" from deck
—House return width = 4'-0"
—Cornice height = 1'-0"
—Cornice depth = 6"

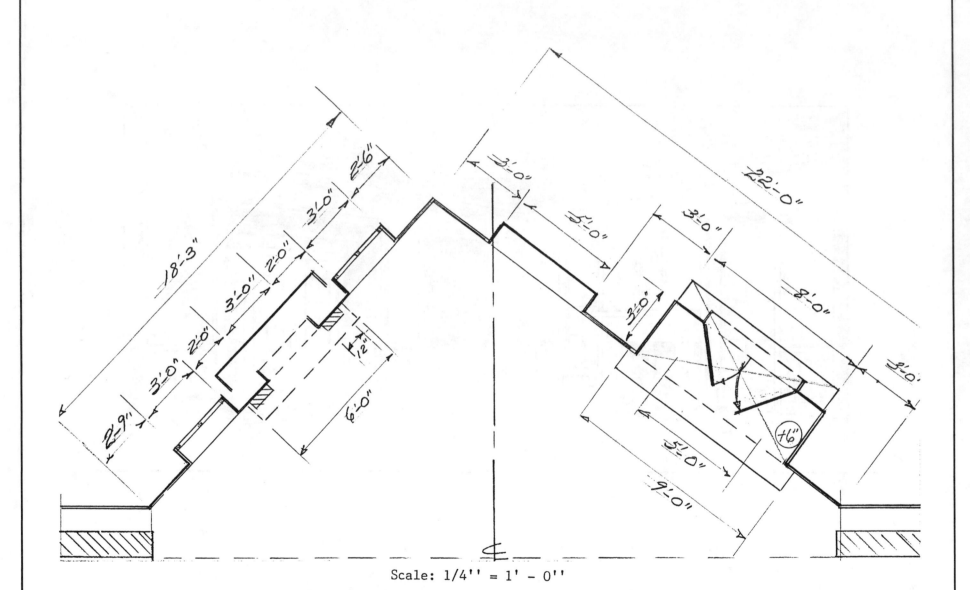

Scale: 1/4'' = 1' - 0''

13. Textures and Materials

On some occasions you may want to draw the textures of the material that you are specifying in your ELEVATIONS. In complicated drawings with lots of different materials, being able to represent the textures accurately can make the illustration clearer and thereby reduce the chance of error. Textures can help the person reading the plans distinguish one object from another. Combined with some shading techniques, texture drawing can help both PLANS and ELEVATIONS appear more dimensional and readable.

Shading Techniques

Using a pencil, a straight edge, and a special shading tool called a stomp, it is possible to create shadows and depth in your drafting. Because it has been shaded, you can get an excellent sense of the platform drawn in the accompanying illustrations. This technique could not be simpler.

1. Hold a straight edge (triangle) down firmly on one edge. Cover the object with the straight edge but leave the pencil line itself uncovered.

2. Take the stomp and rub it back and forth along the edge a few times. If it is a high platform you need a bigger shadow. Slowly move the straight edge away from the edge as you continue to swipe back and forth with the stomp.

3. Continue this process with each side. Instead of a straight edge you can also use 3M "Post-it" brand tape. It will mask the object and then pull up easily without ripping your vellum.

4. For very large shaded areas or brand new stomps you will need to help the stomp by first laying down some graphite shading. Take the side of your pencil and carefully draw in some shading. Go over this with the stomp and a straight edge to smooth it out. You should never be aware of any stomp or pencil strokes.

Graphite sticks work nicely for this type of shading also. They are available at drafting, drawing, or art supply stores. A box of six 4B Kimberly brand graphite sticks should cost you about $4.25.

The stomp shading technique can be used for all sorts of drawings. A single swipe of the stomp below a cornice molding will create a subtle shadow that instantly communicates depth to the carpenters. A swipe around the door trim will graphically demonstrate molding detail applied to the flat.

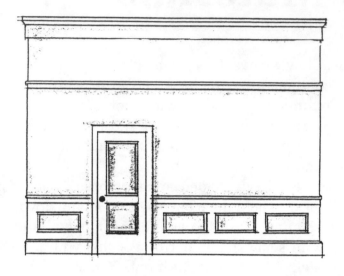

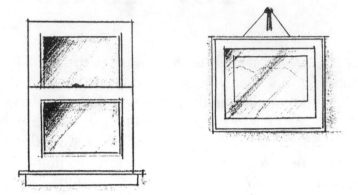

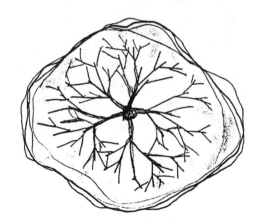

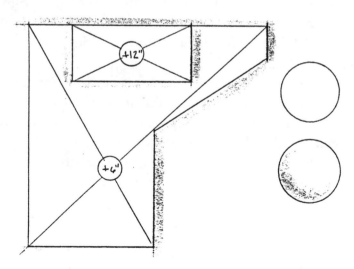

Material Texture Techniques

With a couple of simple tricks, a boring rectangle with a leader note can become a highly textured, very believable brick wall.

As a first step, you will need to have lots of texture examples handy. Never draw a texture from an idea in your head of what the texture is supposed to look like. It will more than likely look phony and amateur. Always have a photo of that material on your drafting board as you are drawing it.

A terrific way to achieve believable texture quite effortlessly in your drafting is to acquire a collection of abundant texture photographs. Before you throw out old magazines, clip out good examples of any wall, fence, or floor treatment. Buy some file folders and file these away. Label each folder by material and perhaps even interior and exterior. In very little time you will have an impressive research morgue that will be the envy of your fellow designers and drafters.

Here are some examples of material texture drawing that were drawn using such a morgue. Included with each example are a couple of hints on what to do and what not to do.

Rough Stone

Be careful not to use too many curved lines. Too many curved lines make the stone look like a storybook castle at best, potatoes at worst. Notice that most of these lines are straight. Show depth by running some broken lines that echo the outline just inside the edge. Shadow the bottom and an edge of each stone slightly with your pencil. Use your stomp to "tone" each stone a bit differently. "Pit" the stone with lots of pencil and stomp taps.

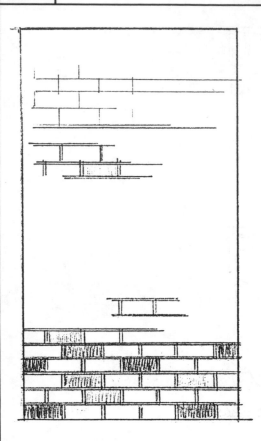

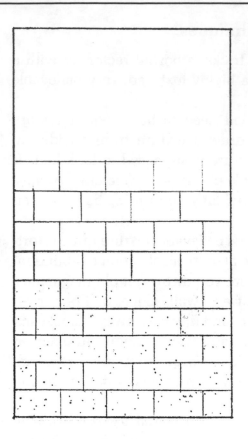

Brick

Show mortar thickness by drawing double lines. Shade each brick a little differently. If you have a large area of brick, fade it out by "suggesting" it in some parts (as in this example). There are many different sizes and varieties of brick. Make sure that the style you choose is appropriate historically and to the region. Size is most important here. Be sure your bricks are of the correct dimension.

Concrete Block

Concrete block can be drawn with a single or a double mortar line. It uses pencil tapping extensively to create its texture. Multiple pencils held in the hand and tapped all at once is a way of speeding this up. To avoid making a tap pattern, twist and rearrange the multiple pencils. The stomp is not needed with this simple material.

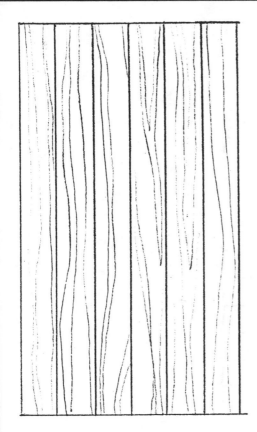

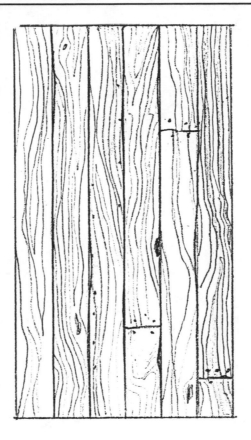

Interior Smooth Wood Paneling or Flooring

The key to a finished lumber look is to not draw knots. Draw all lines of grain in pairs. Notice that these are all drawn in sets of two. Each grain line should begin and end at an end or edge. We should never see an arbitrary beginning or end of any grain inside the paneling. Use the stomp to shade inside an occasional pair of grain lines on some boards and most pairs on others. Use variety for a natural look. Avoid predictable and repeating patterns.

Rough Lumber

For a rougher look introduce knots. But be careful, don't draw cartoon knots. Refer to your research. Generally you will have more grain lines and they will have more change of direction. For emphasis, butt joints, lines, and nail heads are helpful if appropriate. Use the stomp in the same way that you would use it for finished lumber. Use some pencil tapping to get a pitted or worm hole look.

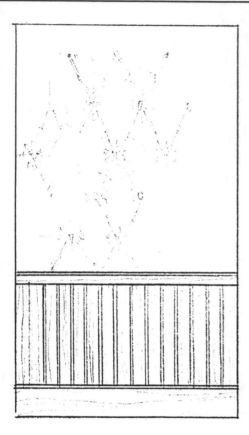

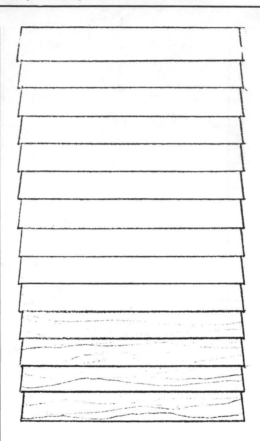

V-Groove Wainscot Paneling with Wallpaper

All of this wood should be grained as you did for the finished paneling. To get the sense of the v-groove draw three vertical lines right next to each other. A curved or square groove paneling would show two lines. The wallpaper should be hinted at and faded out. This would be too time consuming if drawn too completely. Use a leader to indicate wallpaper. Draw it in only when it might clear up a complicated drawing.

Clapboard

The trick to clapboard is to draw the angled edges. Another help is to swipe it with the stomp just below each horizontal line (a straight edge is essential). Some of the finished paneling techniques should be used. Use very little for a freshly painted siding. Use a lot for older weathered and peeling clapboard. Never use the rough lumber technique here.

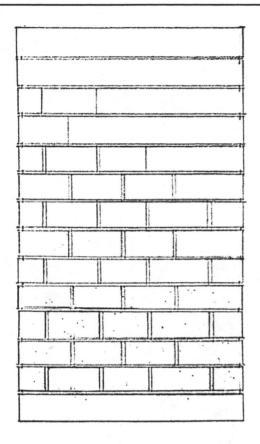

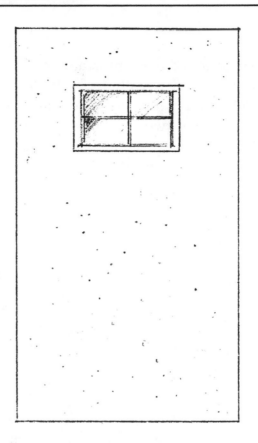

Cut Stone

Drawing a double mortar line is crucial when drawing cut stone. Use the pencil tapping technique to create some stone texture. Use the stomp to *subtly* shade some or most of the stones (not half). Fade out and suggest stone if you have a lot to do and need to save time.

Concrete

An easy technique—accomplished primarily with the pencil tapping method. Be sure to always twist your hand in different positions if you are holding a number of pencils. This prevents a pattern from forming on the surface. Draw cracks only if called for within the character of the setting. Refer to research for an authentic look.

Glass

Start with your pencil in a corner and draw back and forth diagonally getting lighter to the touch with each stroke. Start dark in the corner and fade out when you have drawn out to about ⅓ of the pane. Draw two or three strokes further into the pane. Add some stomp shading. Begin at the dark corner and fade out at about two-thirds of the way into the pane. This takes some practice but can yield a convincing result.

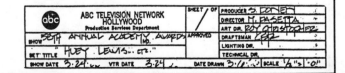

ELEVATION from the 58th Academy Awards (Television) showing extensive stomp shading to give fullness to the curtains.

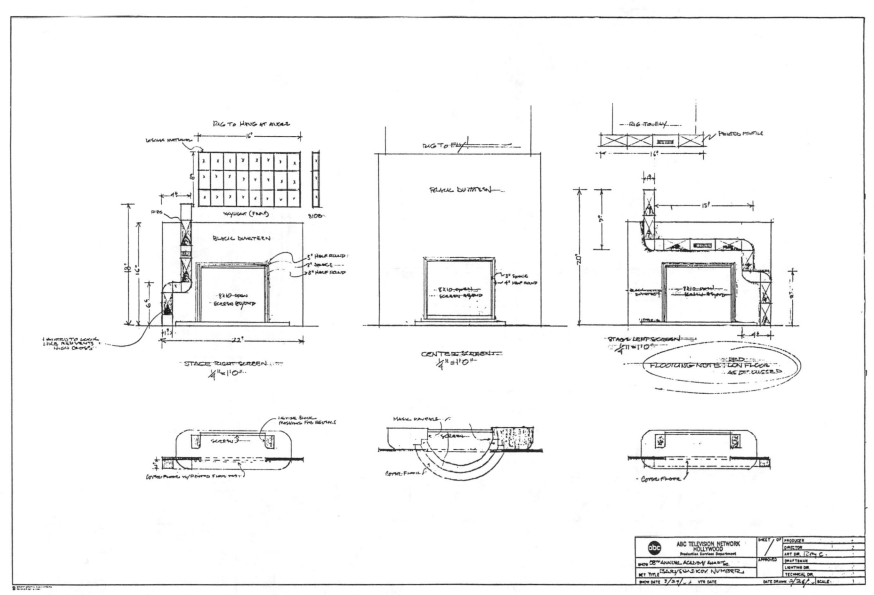

ELEVATION from the 58th Academy Awards (Television) showing extensive stomp shading to give depth to the scenic pieces.

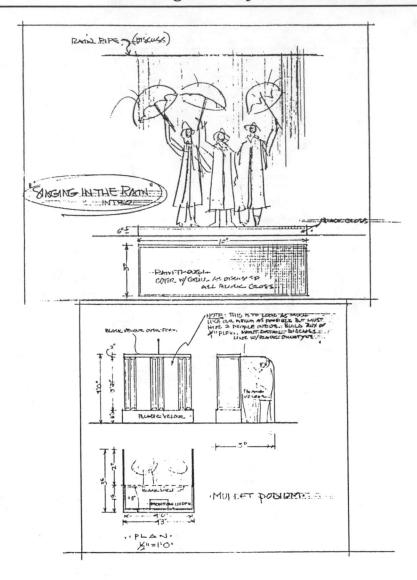

ELEVATION from the 58th Academy Awards (Television) showing the use of human figures for scale and stomp shading to give the sense of a smoke (liquid nitrogen) effect.

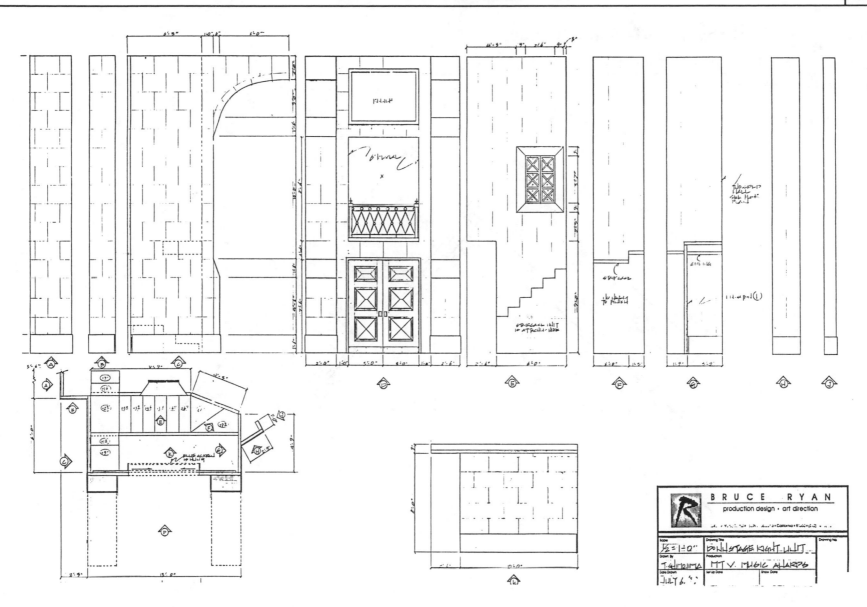

ELEVATION from the MTV Awards (Television) using a cut stone texture throughout.

Project 11 Drafting Materials and Textures

1. Draft a set of <u>FRONT ELEVATIONS</u> only, for the set sketched on the next sheet.

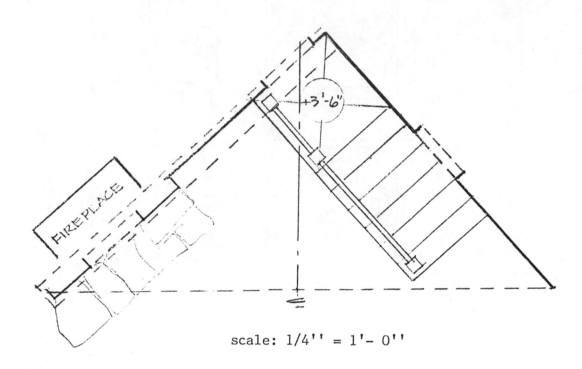

scale: 1/4'' = 1'- 0''

2. SPECIFICATIONS:

—The 3″ chair rail is 3′ from the floor.
—Base board is 6″ high.
—All other molding is 5″ wide.
—Fireplace apron is 3″ high.
—All walls are 12′ high.

—The beam is 1′ square.
—Hand rail is 2′-6″ high.
—Center wall is wallpaper above v-groove paneling.
—Window is 4′-6″ high and 2′ from top of wall.
—Fireplace lintel is 4′ long and 6″ high.

14. True Shape and Size

This sketch is from a portion of a set design for the Sanskrit drama *Sakuntala*. A major visual element of the set is the double-slanted roof.

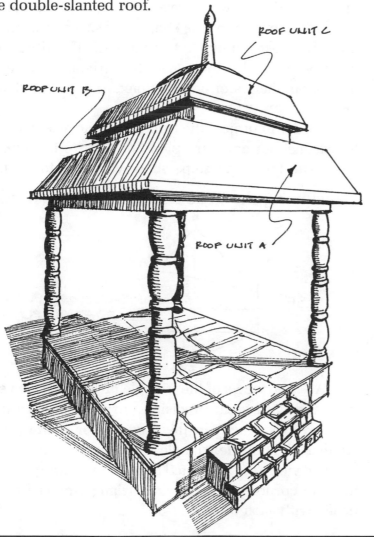

ROOF UNIT C

ROOF UNIT B

ROOF UNIT A

Askew, Oblique, and Inclined

A problem in drafting this roof for the scene shop was that neither a FRONT ELEVATION nor a PLAN would show us the actual shape of the roof. You see, up until now we have been working with views of scenic elements that neatly fit into one of two categories. These two categories are the principal picture planes of orthographic projection.

The first category is the picture plane that is parallel to the FLOOR PLAN. When developing a FLOOR PLAN the draftsperson takes the elements on the stage and projects them right up and into the parallel FLOOR PLAN picture plane. A wall that is 10′ long on the stage (in scale) appears as a 10′ long line on the PLAN and is measurable with a scale rule.

Perpendicular to this plane is the other category. This other category contains the infinite number of planes that are projected onto one of these planes and then is drafted as an ELEVATION. A 15′ high wall of the set appears as a 15′ high wall on the ELEVATION and is measurable with a scale rule as well. If you look at the slanted roof units A and C, you see that neither roof is parallel or perpendicular to the stage floor. Views of the roof projected onto a PLAN or an ELEVATION would depict foreshortened shapes. Now, the top and bottom edges of the roof would be correct. They would be showing their true *length*. All four of those lines conform to the planes of normal orthographic projection because they are parallel to one of the planes

(FLOOR PLAN plane). The slanted sides, however, would not be true length. These lines are *askew* (oblique or inclined); they are neither parallel nor perpendicular to the stage floor.

Before we could draw an undistorted ELEVATION of the roof units, we had to determine the *true shape and size.*

Descriptive Geometry

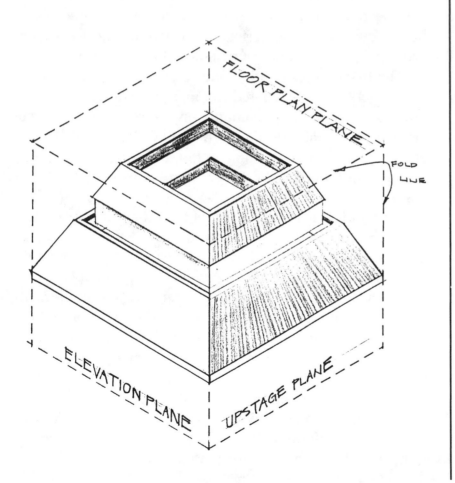

In the drawing above you see one of the *Sakuntala* roof units floating inside a cube. We are now dealing with an area of mathematics called descriptive geometry. The cube represents the principal planes of projection. On each surface of the cube you can almost see the PLAN or ELEVATION of the roof projected on it. Remember now that these would be false views, foreshortened because the surfaces are inclined (askew) in relation to the projection planes.

To determine the true shape and size of a scenic unit it must be broken down into triangles. The *Sakuntala* roof must be divided into at least two triangles. The two triangles can then later be assembled to reveal the true shape and size.

In order to project the true shape and size, we will need to establish an auxiliary plane parallel to the pitch of the roof. The following steps show you how to do just that.

Developing the True Shape and Size (Method 1)

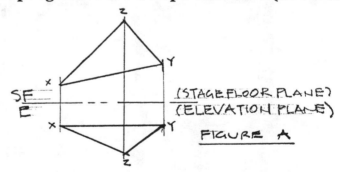

FIG A—Two views of the triangle must be set up very carefully and with great precision. In this case we have one of the views drawn in the Stage Floor Plane (SF) above another view of the triangle from the Elevation (E) plane. The two views are separated by the view folding line. Notice that the corner points of each triangle must line up vertically with each other.

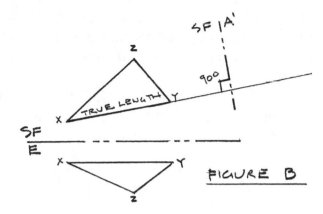

FIGURE B

FIG. B—In the Stage Floor Plane, extend XY out to the right and establish the SF-A1 (Auxiliary Plane 1) fold line perpendicular to the true length. In this case XY is a true length because it is parallel to the fold line in the other view.

NOTE: If a line is parallel to the folding line, then the folded view adjacent to it shows its true length! If you're not convinced by that, examine Figure A to find an example of this statement.

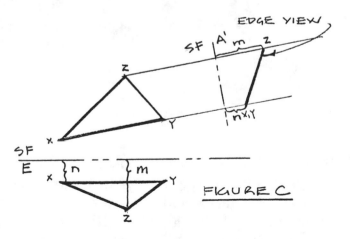

FIGURE C

FIG. C—Draw a line parallel to the XY extension that originates at point Z. Plot points X, Y, and Z as shown. Notice that to do this accurately distance n must equal distance n and distance m must equal distance m. This establishes an edge view.

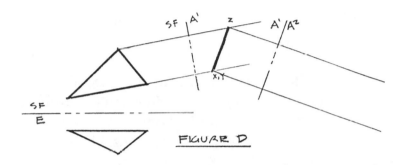

FIGURE D

FIG. D—In A1 (Auxiliary Plane 1), draw a line perpendicular to line XYZ from point Z and a line parallel to it from points X, Y. These lines should continue off to the right. A short distance away from the edge view draw a folding line parallel to the edge view. This folding line will separate A1 from A2.

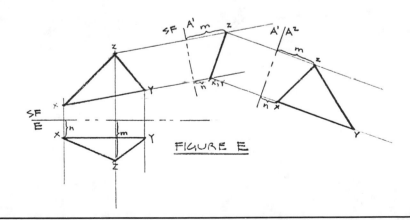

FIGURE E

FIG E—Now we can establish the true shape and size. Plot point X. Its distance away from the A1 A2 folding line is n. Plot point Z. Its distance away from the folding line is m. The distance from X to Y is the true length distance established in Figure B. This new shape XYZ is the true size and shape of the object.

Remember that for objects with more than three sides, you will need to break them up into triangles, find the true size and shape of each, and then assemble them into the true shapes.

In the example we just examined, we were able to establish the true length of one of the sides quite effortlessly. This was due to the fact that we had one of the sides of one of the triangles positioned parallel to the folding line. In some <u>PLAN</u> and <u>ELEVATION</u> drawing pairs, no side of the object will be parallel to a projection plane. In these situations you must solve for true shape and size using a variation of the technique just demonstrated.

Developing the True Shape and Size When No Side Is Parallel to the Folding Line Using Method 1

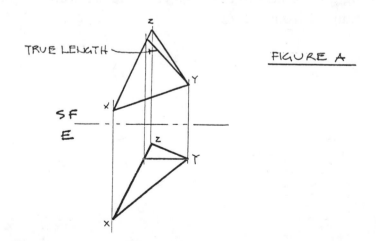

FIGURE A

FIG A—Again, line up the two views very carefully. To get a true line length, draw a horizontal line in the Elevation Plane from one corner to the other side, as we did here by drawing a line from Y to side XZ. Draw a line 90° up from that point. Where it crosses side XZ in the stage floor plane is the point where the end of the line will be in that view. In the SF view, connect that new point with Y to get the true length.

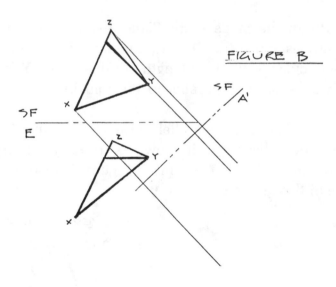

FIGURE B

FIG B—Extend the true length line out and to the right. Establish a fold line perpendicular to the true length extension. Extend points X and Z out across the folding line as well by drawing lines parallel to the true length extension from those two points.

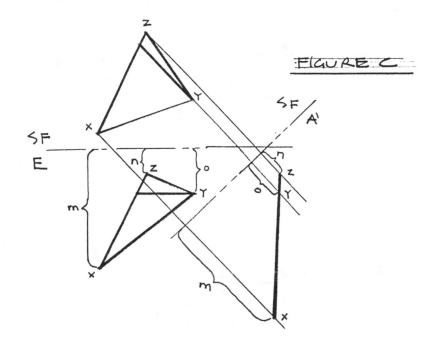

FIGURE C

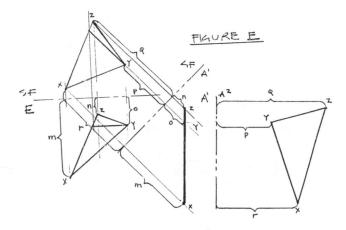

FIGURE E

FIG C—Establish the edge view. Notice that to do this accurately, distance m must equal distance m, distance n must equal distance n, and distance o must equal distance o.

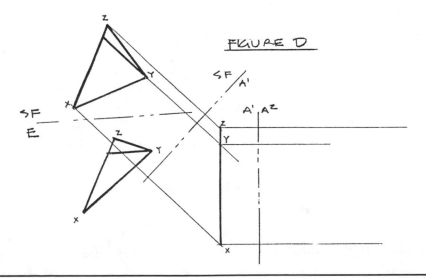

FIGURE D

FIG D—In A1, a short distance away from the edge view, draw a folding line parallel to the edge view. This folding line will separate A1 from A2. From points X, Y, and Z on the edge view draw three lines perpendicular to this view. These three parallel lines should go off to the right.

FIG E—Now we can establish the true shape and size. Plot point X. Its distance away from the A1 A2 folding line is r. Plot point Z. Its distance away from the folding line is q. The distance from Y to the folding line is p. This new shape XYZ is the true size and shape of the object.

Remember that here too, for objects with more than three sides, you will need to break them up into triangles, find the true size and shape of each, and then assemble them into the true shapes.

Developing the True Shape and Size (Method 2)

This alternative method for determining the true size and shape requires that you first determine the true length of each side. This is done by rotating each side until it is parallel to the folding line in one view and then adjusting it in the other view. This adjusted view is the true length.

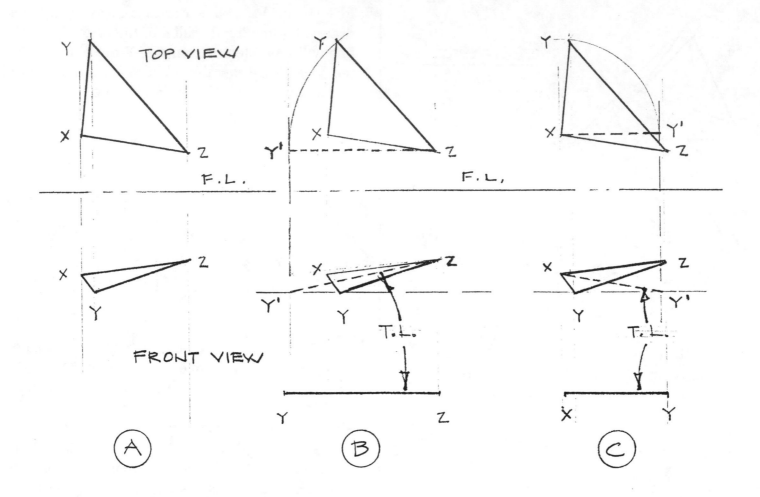

FIG A—Carefully line up the two views

FIG B—With a compass rotate YZ until it is parallel to the folding line (F.L.). Adjust the same line in the other view by:

1. extending Y1 down past the triangle in the lower view
2. drawing a line parallel to the folding line through point Y in the lower view intersecting with a line drawn in the previous step (new point Y1)

Draw a line from Z to Y1 in the lower view. This is the true length of the line.

FIG C—Repeat the above steps to find the true length of XY.

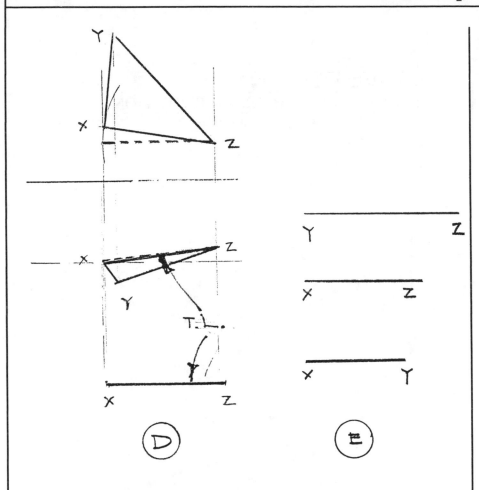

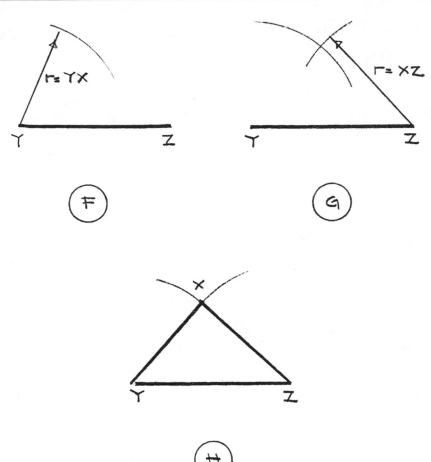

FIG D—Find the true length of XZ.

FIG E—Draw the true lengths of the three line segments.

FIG F—Draw one of the segments as a base. Using the radius of one of the other lines, draw an arc at one end.

FIG G—Do the same at the other end of the base using the last line as the radius.

FIG H—Draw in the other two sides of the triangle by drawing lines from the two ends of the base to the intersection of the arcs. This is the true shape of triangle XYZ.

Project 12   True Shape and Size

1. Draw your border.
2. Lay out your title block.
3. Below are the <u>PLAN</u> and <u>FRONT ELEVATION</u> of various shapes. Determine and draw the true size and shape of each shape.
4. Show your work. Draw the following three views:

   a. <u>PLAN VIEW</u>
   b. <u>FRONT ELEVATION</u>
   c. <u>TRUE SIZE AND SHAPE ELEVATION</u>
5. Line the views up vertically.
6. Fully label each view.
7. Finish your title block.

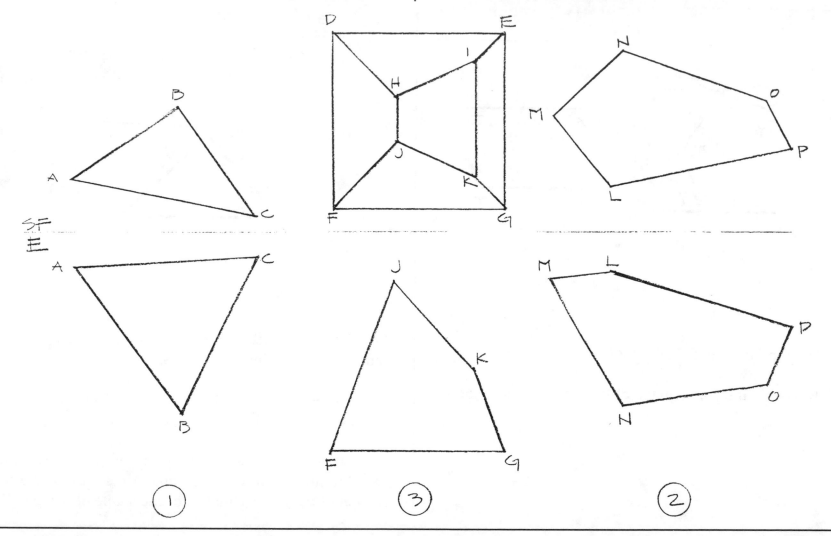

Project 13   True Shape and Size

1. Draw your border.
2. Lay out your title block.
3. Below and on the next page are the <u>PLAN</u> and <u>FRONT ELEVATION</u> of the *Sakuntala* roof unit. Determine and draw the true size and shape of side 1 roof unit A (½" scale).
4. Show your work. Draw the following three views:

a. <u>PLAN VIEW</u>
b. <u>FRONT ELEVATION</u>
c. <u>TRUE SIZE AND SHAPE ELEVATION</u>
5. Line up the views vertically.
6. Fully label each view and dimension the true shape <u>ELEVATION</u>.
7. Finish your title block.

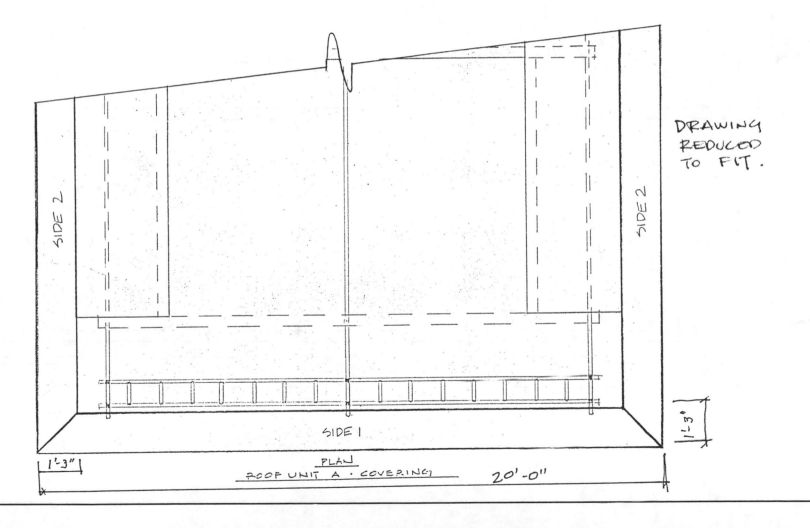

DRAWING REDUCED TO FIT.

SIDE 2

SIDE 2

SIDE 1

1'-3"

PLAN
ROOF UNIT A · COVERING

1'-3"

20'-0"

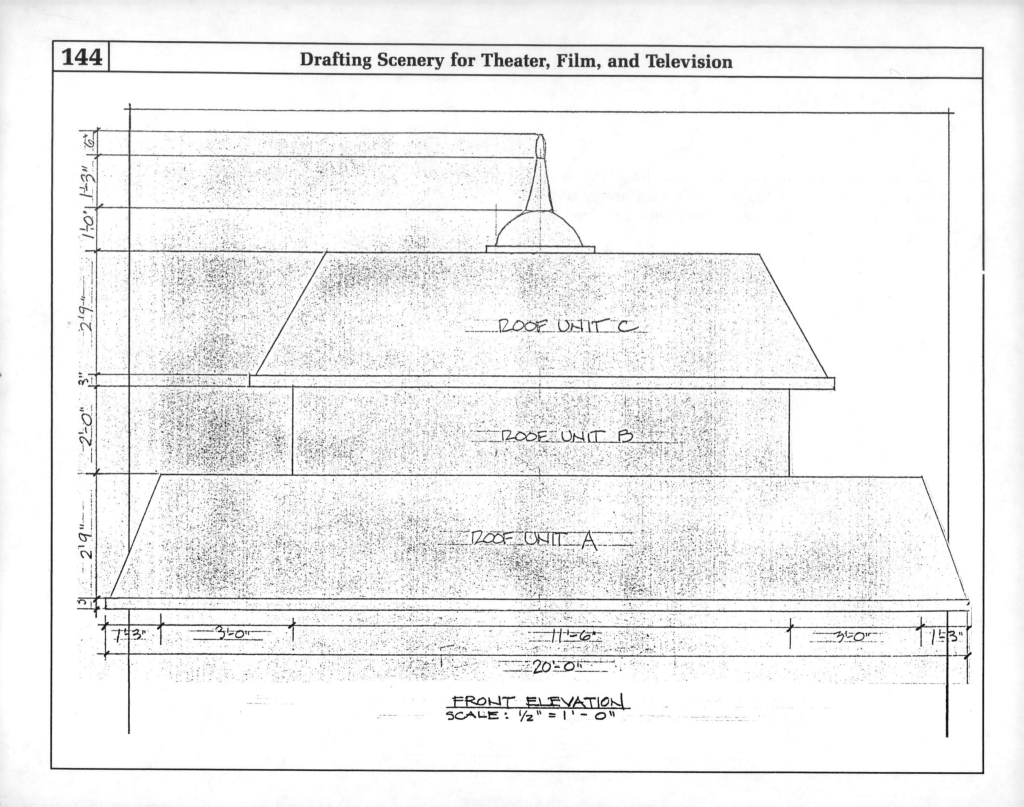

ROOF UNIT C

ROOF UNIT B

ROOF UNIT A

6"

1'-3"

1'-0"

2'-9"

3"

2'-0"

2'-9"

3"

1'-3" 3'-0" 11'-6" 3'-0" 1'-3"

20'-0"

FRONT ELEVATION
SCALE: 1/2" = 1' - 0"

15. True Curve

Below and at right are an ELEVATION and PLAN of a 16th century garden house. The roof piece of this garden house presents a major drafting problem. The roof support pieces need to be drafted, yet they are curved and are not parallel to the folding line in any of the views. No view shows the true curve. They are quite foreshortened in the ELEVATION as well as the PLAN.

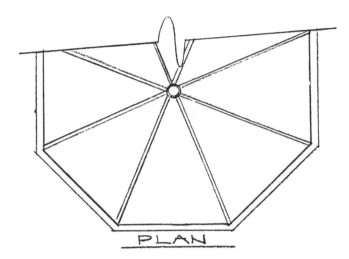

PLAN

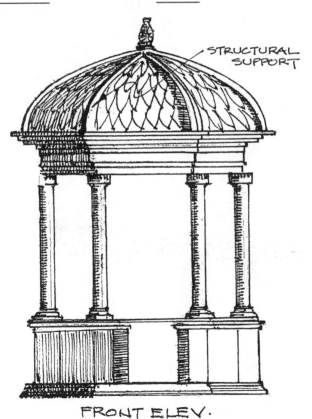

STRUCTURAL SUPPORT

FRONT ELEV.

Just as the true length of foreshortened sides must be determined in order to draw a true shape, the true curve of these supports must be established before they can be drafted in a CONSTRUCTION ELEVATION.

Besides establishing a correct roof line, finding the true curve could also be helpful for drafting such problem scenic elements as lamp shades, architectural domes, umbrellas, 3-D rocks, hills, and more.

On the next few pages are the steps you must follow to find the true curve of an object that is askew.

Determining the True Curve

1. After aligning the PLAN and ELEVATION, draw a line through the center of the PLAN view, parallel to the folding line.

2. Divide up half of this line, in increments and spacing of your choosing. The more increments the more accurate the results will be.

3. Extend these points down to the first support they hit in the <u>PLAN</u>. Mark these points.

4. Continue these extensions down to the <u>ELEVATION</u> at the first support and then right across to the center line.

5. Draw a cross axis somewhere else on your vellum and plot:

    a. on the vertical axis, the points marked on the center line

    b. on the horizontal axis, the points marked on the first <u>PLAN</u> support in step 3.

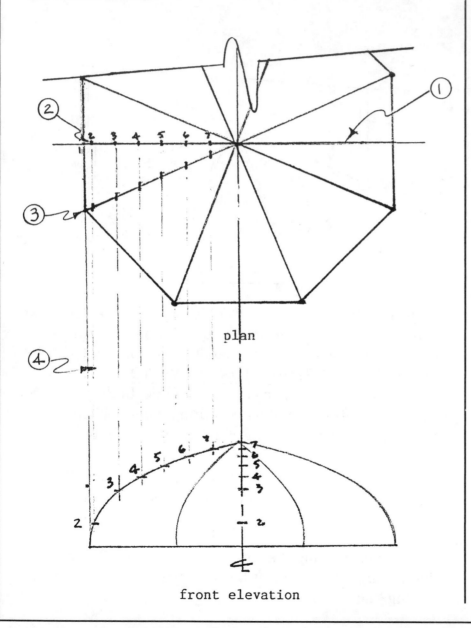

plan

front elevation

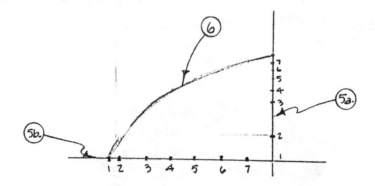

true curve cross axis

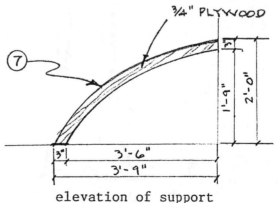

elevation of support

6. Grid these points on the cross axis. Mark where each point intersects. Connect these points to reveal the true curve of the supports.

7. Using the curve, draw an ELEVATION of the support.

Project 14 True Curve

1. Find a 4, 5, 6, 7, or 8 sided prop or scenic element with a curved top.

2. Draw your border.

3. Lay out your title block.

4. Draw a PLAN and a FRONT ELEVATION of your prop. Be sure to line them up vertically. Also make sure that one of the sides is parallel to the folding line.

5. Develop the true curve for one of the supports.

6. Draw a DETAIL in a larger size of one of the supports.

7. Fully label, identify materials to be used, and dimension the support.

8. Show your work. Include your dropped points and cross axis.

9. Finish your title block.

16. Axonometrics and Obliques

With some very intricate objects such as props or three-dimensional scenic pieces, you may discover that the ELEVATION view flattens things out too much, and adding more DETAIL views can just be too confusing. You may find that you need to give the person responsible for the construction of the object a more realistic sense of the dimensionality.

In these situations it is helpful to provide a more pictorial view. There are three categories of pictorial drawings in the fields of engineering and architecture; AXONOMETRIC, OBLIQUE, and PERSPECTIVE. SECTIONS 16 and 17 will examine the most common of the three AXONOMETRIC drawings (the ISOMETRIC), both of the OBLIQUE drawings (CAVALIER and CABINET), and PERSPECTIVE.

Both AXONOMETRIC and OBLIQUE drawings show three sides of the object in a manner closer to a sketch than it is to an ELEVATION. But unlike a sketch, these views are drawn with precision, drafted to a scale, and are therefore measurable. The trade-off of not having the perspective of a sketch is that the object will appear somewhat distorted in any AXONOMETRIC or OBLIQUE drawing.

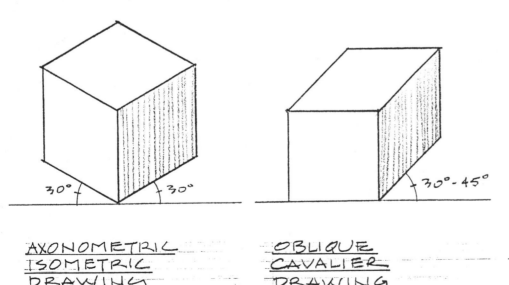

AXONOMETRIC
ISOMETRIC
DRAWING

OBLIQUE
CAVALIER
DRAWING

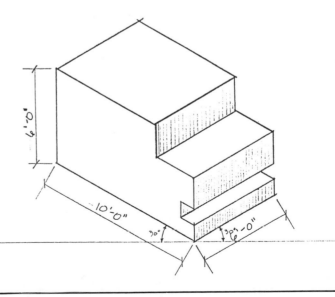

Axonometric Isometric Drawing

Of the three (actually four) pictorial techniques that we will look at, the AXONOMETRIC distorts the object the least. There are three types of AXONOMETRIC drawings; the ISOMETRIC, the TRIMETRIC, and the DIMETRIC. Each is a slight variation on the other.

As you can see above, the AXONOMETRIC drawing places one *edge* of the object on an imaginary reference plane called the picture plane. Think of the picture plane as an imaginary sheet of glass. The edge rests on an imaginary baseline drawn on the picture plane. The two lines representing the bottom of the object are both drawn at an angle to the baseline.

For the ISOMETRIC DRAWING each side is drawn at 30°.

For the TRIMETRIC DRAWING the left side is drawn at 15° and the right side is drawn at 45°.

For the DIMETRIC DRAWING each side is drawn at 15°.

In theatrical drawing, the ISOMETRIC is the most common. All vertical lines remain vertical on the ISOMETRIC. Lines of depth that are parallel to the bottom of the object all run at 30°.

The object is drawn completely to scale. Any line that is either perpendicular to the baseline or at 30° can be measured with a scale rule. Other lines in the drawing, however, are foreshortened and cannot be scaled.

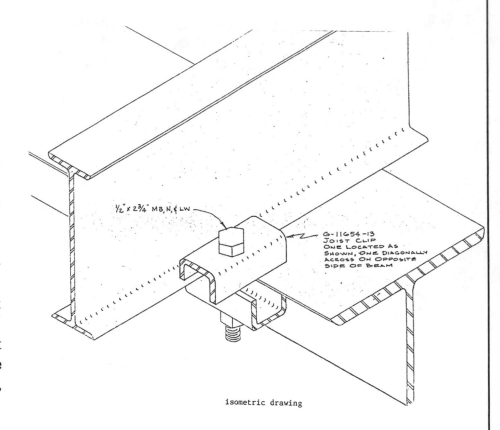

½" x 2¾" MB, N, ¢ LW

G-11654-13
JOIST CLIP
ONE LOCATED AS
SHOWN, ONE DIAGONALLY
ACROSS ON OPPOSITE
SIDE OF BEAM

isometric drawing

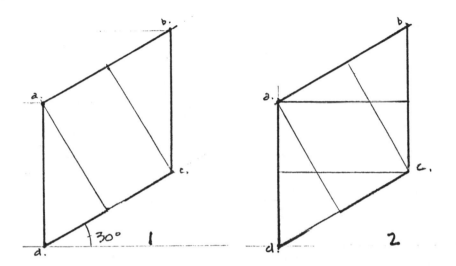
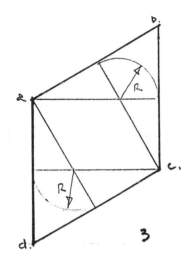
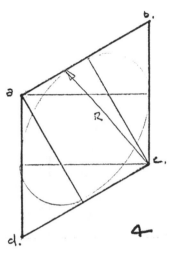

Isometric Circle

Drawing a circle on an <u>ISOMETRIC</u> can be quite a difficult task. These steps will greatly simplify the process.

1. Draw a line going from corner a to line dc. The line must meet dc at the mid-point.

Draw a line going from corner c to line ab. The line must meet ab at the mid-point.

2. Draw a line going from corner a to line bc. The line must meet bc at the mid-point.

3. At the intersection of each pair of lines, draw an arc using the length of the line segment (past the point of inter-section) as the radius.

4. At points a and c draw an arc connecting the two arcs that you just drew. For the radius use the length of one of the lines drawn in step 1.

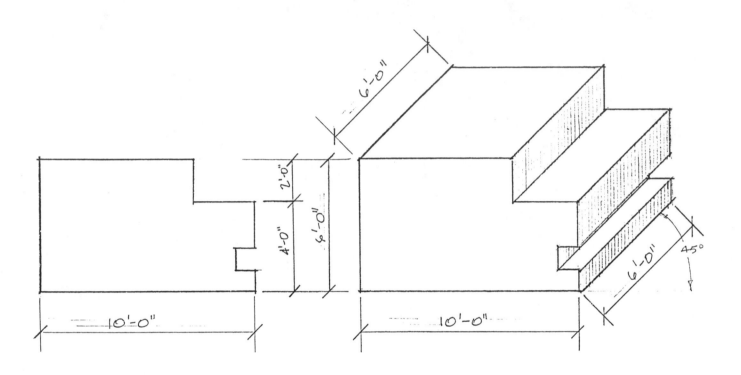

OBLIQUE Drawing

The next pictorial drawing technique that we will explain is the OBLIQUE drawing. There are two types of OBLIQUE drawings, the CAVALIER and the CABINET. When developing an OBLIQUE drawing you must place one *side* of the object on the picture plane. You should choose the most intricate or complicated side to place on the picture plane. The other line that represents the bottom of the object is drawn at 30°–45° to the baseline. Like the AXONOMET-RIC ISOMETRIC, the CAVALIER drawing is made to scale and is measurable as long as the line being measured is parallel or perpendicular to the baseline or is parallel to one of the sides. The OBLIQUE CAVALIER is the most distorted drawing of all of the pictorial techniques. The depth appears to be much greater than it really is. A cube will appear to be an elongated box. For this reason it is the least desirable drawing method to use.

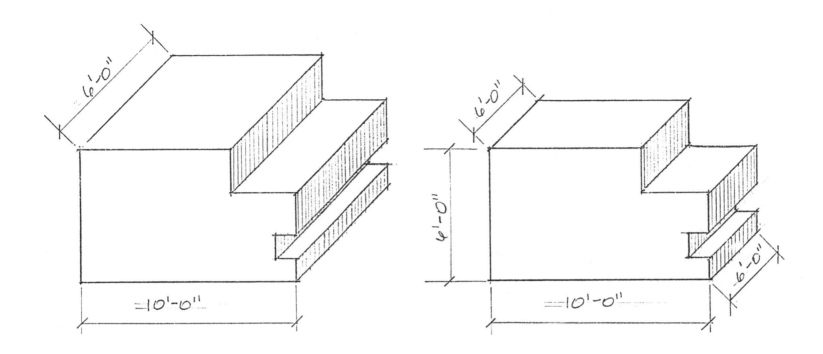

OBLIQUE CABINET Drawing

This variation of the OBLIQUE drawing helps solve the depth distortion problem. The technique used to accomplish this is to compress the depth of the object into half the space. A 6′ depth is drawn in 3 scale feet. As you can imagine, it is quite important to label an OBLIQUE CABINET as such. You may even want to make a note pointing out the fact that the depth is drawn at half the intended length. It is extremely important to dimension every line of depth also. If a carpenter were to take a scale rule to the object and measure 3′ it could lead to a catastrophic error in construction.

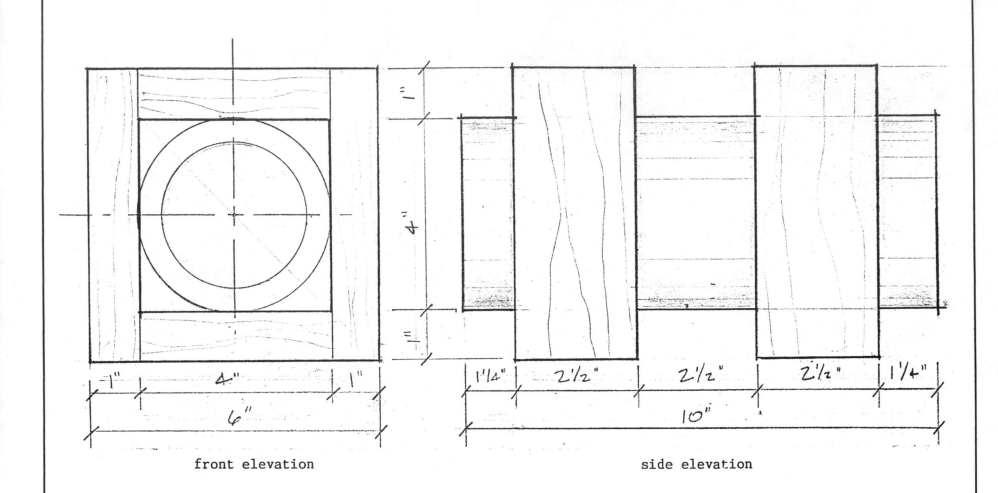

front elevation   side elevation

Project 15   AXONOMETRIC ISOMETRICS

1. Draw your border.
2. Lay out your title block.
3. Draw an <u>AXONOMETRIC ISOMETRIC</u> of the object (FULL SCALE). Include shading and texture if you have time.

4. Finish your title block.

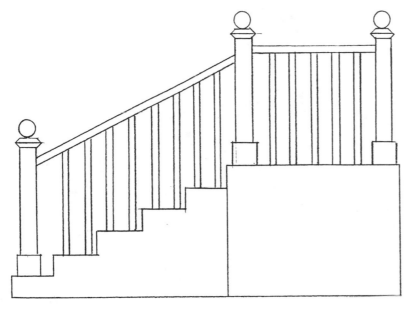

side elevation

(scale: 1/2'' = 1'– 0'')

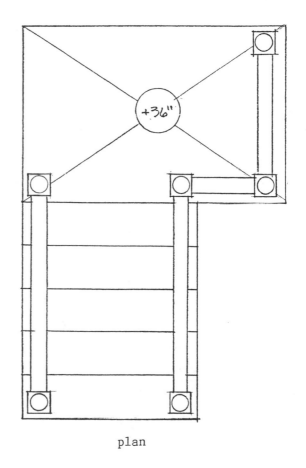

plan

Project 16 OBLIQUE CABINET

1. Draw your border.
2. Lay out your title block.
3. Draw an <u>OBLIQUE CABINET</u> of this object (1″ SCALE). Include shading and texture if you have time.
4. Finish your title block.

17. Perspective Sketch

"IN THE SWEET BYE & BYE"
ROUGH SKETCH

for DONALD DRIVER
BACK ALLEY THEATER

A blueprint of a perspective sketch is an excellent way of prefacing the working drawings. It is a constant, easily accessible, visual reminder of the setting to those building the set.

So much the better if you have the drawing skills required to produce such a sketch. Many draftspersons need assistance however. Traditional perspective sketching is a method whereby an accurate drawing is developed mechanically and mathematically using numerous steps which extrapolate information from the <u>FLOOR PLAN</u>. There are a multitude of mechanical perspective methods available. Dozens of them have been adapted for use in scenery sketching. The majority of these methods are so complex and intricate that many draftspersons simply stay away from them altogether. The word perspective alone seems to strike fear in so many that they lose the aptitude to assimilate the necessary information in these elaborate methods.

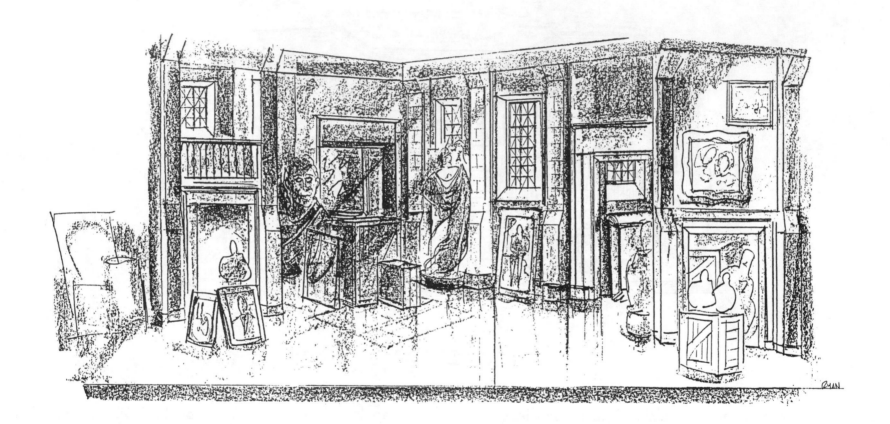

6TH MTV VIDEO MUSIC AWARDS

Pencil and graphite stick <u>PERSPECTIVE SKETCH</u>
for the 6th MTV Awards show (Television).

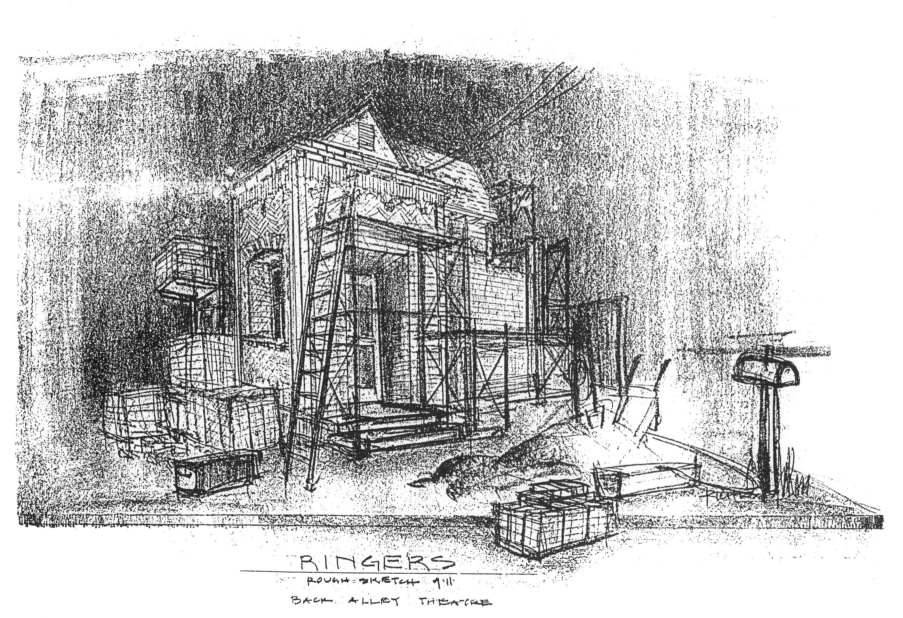

RINGERS
ROUGH SKETCH 9'11'
BACK ALLEY THEATRE

Pencil <u>PERSPECTIVE SKETCH</u> for *Ringers* (Theater).

What follows here is a gathering of various aspects gleaned from many of these traditional perspective methods. You will find that the steps presented here are fewer than those found in other methods and simpler to understand. The resulting sketch of your set may not be as accurate as it would be from one of the more mysterious and traditional methods, but you will find it a friendlier system with quick, very good results. If as a result of this method you find some of your sketch is too distorted, it is a simple matter to go over the sketch and touch it up.

This system entails that you draft a ⅜″ FLOOR PLAN of the set portion of your PLAN. You will place this PLAN at the top of your drafting table and then develop the rendering directly below it. You will need a lot of vertical space on your drafting table.

1. Draw the PLAN in ⅜″ scale near the top of your sheet. Extend the center line of the PLAN all the way down to the bottom of the sheet.

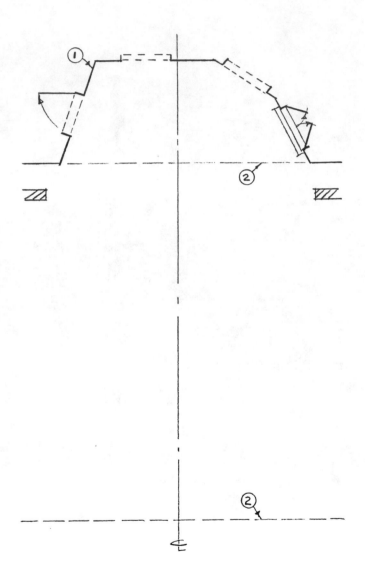

2. Establish the set line on your <u>FLOOR PLAN</u> *and* at the bottom of the sheet.

3. Starting at the center line of your <u>PLAN</u> and moving offstage in both directions, mark off 1″ increments along the upper set line until you have covered the set.

Draw vertical lines starting with the center line marked 0. Work your way off stage in both directions.

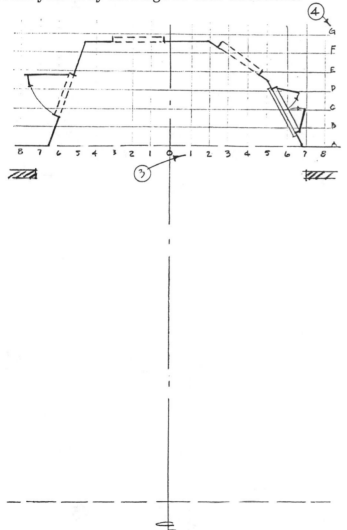

4. To complete the upper grid, mark off 1″ increments along the outermost vertical line.

Draw horizontal lines that start at these marks and go across the <u>FLOOR PLAN</u>.

Label these lines starting with "A" at the set line working upstage.

5. Draw a horizon line in the lower part of your sheet. This line will be parallel to your set line and represents the eye level of a person sitting in the center of the audience.

You can determine the height of this line by examining a <u>CENTER LINE VERTICAL SECTION</u> of the theater. You can also "rough in" its position by drawing it about 3 or 4 ³⁄₈″ scale feet above the set line.

The intersection of the horizon line and the center line is the center vanishing point (c.v.p.).

6. Establish an observation point (o.p.) along the center line at about the middle of the audience.

7. Draw lines from the o.p. to 6A, 6B, 6C, etc. on the upper grid.

8. Drop the points numbered along the upper set line down to the lower set line.

9. Connect each of these dropped set-line points to the c.v.p.

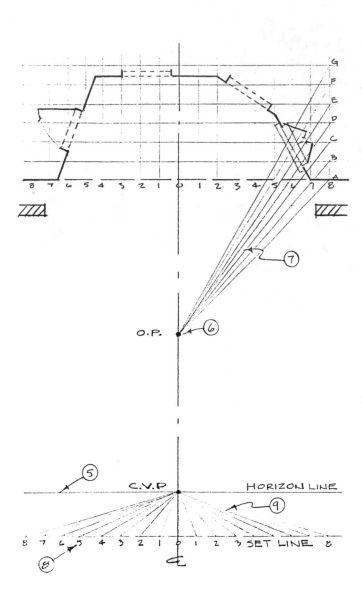

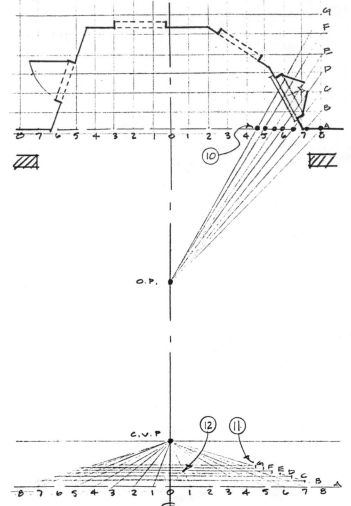

10. Mark along the upper set line where the marks that we drew from the o.p. intersect with the set line.

11. Drop these points straight down to the outermost line on the lower grid (c.v.p. 8).

12. Draw lines parallel to the lower set line across the lower drawing to form a grid.

Start these lines at the points you just dropped from the upper drawing.

13. Draw the <u>PLAN</u> on the lower grid by comparing and dropping the points at which the set walls intersect the upper grid.

14. Draw in the walls of the set. Draw walls only at this time. Other details such as door and window openings will be drawn in later.

15. Begin drawing in the tops of the set walls.

a. Using your ⅜″ scale, mark the desired height of the set walls that are on the set line. In this case the walls will be 12′.

b. Establish the vanishing point for the stage right wall. This point is the intersection of the horizon line and an imaginary extension of that wall.

c. Draw a line going from the edge of the stage right wall which is on the set line. Draw the line starting from the desired height and ending at the next wall line. The line should go toward the vanishing point for that wall.

16. Establish the vanishing points for the other walls and draw in the tops of the walls for the remainder of the set.

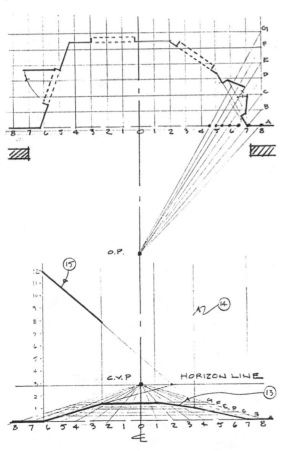

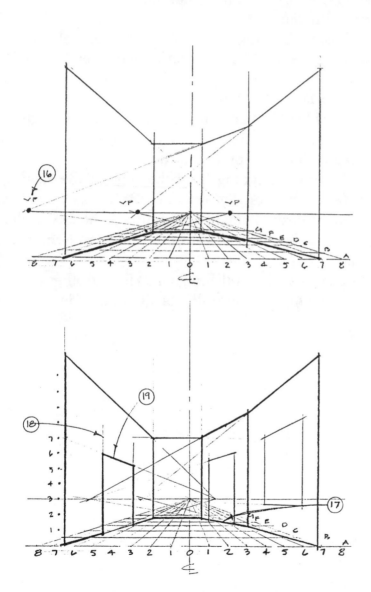

17. On the grid, establish the openings of windows, doors, etc.

18. Draw vertical lines representing the sides of all of these openings.

19. Draw in the tops and bottoms of these openings.

This is done by measuring from a wall on the set line in ⅜″ scale, the desired height of the particular opening. Next, you draw across the walls, heading toward the vanishing point for each wall.

20. Trace the sketch onto a sheet of vellum and draw in all of the details.

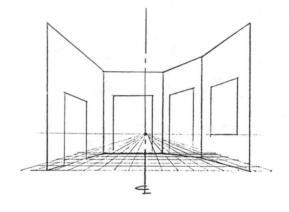

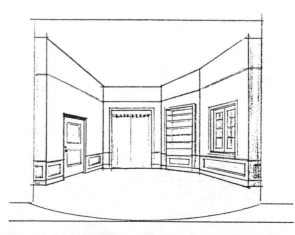

Project 17   PERSPECTIVE SKETCH

1. On a worksheet, draw a perspective sketch from a
FLOOR PLAN.
2. On a sheet of vellum, draw a border.
3. Lay out your title box.
4. Trace your perspective sketch onto your vellum.
5. Add detail and shading.
6. Finish your title block.

Pencil and graphite stick PERSPECTIVE SKETCH
for the 5th MTV Awards show (Television).

Pencil and graphite stick PERSPECTIVE SKETCH
for the American Comedy Awards show (Television).

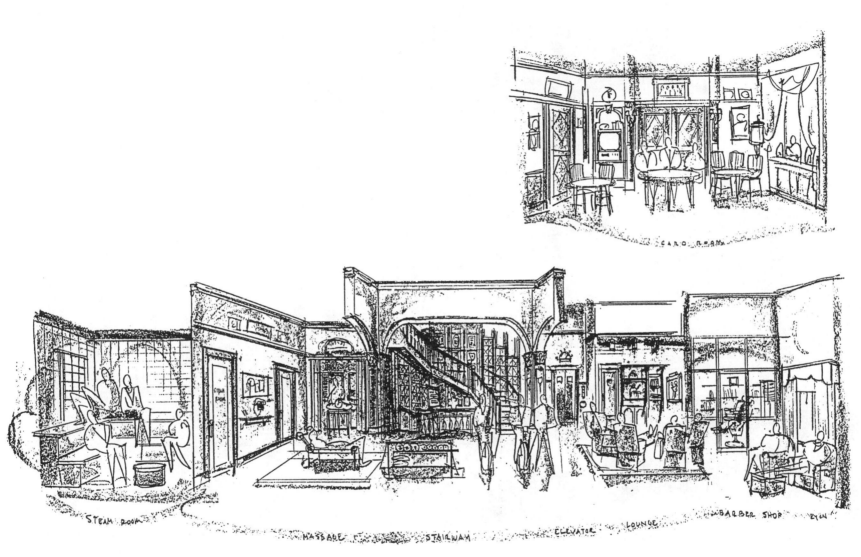

Pencil and graphite stick PERSPECTIVE SKETCH
for *The Boys* (Television).

THE LOBBY AND BAR

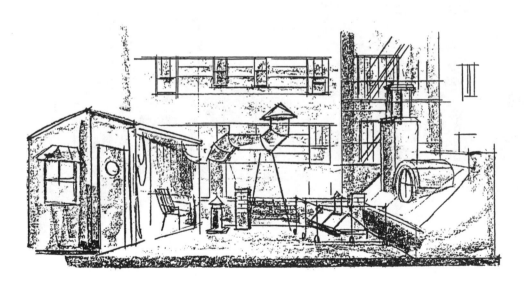

THE APARTMENT

THE ROOFTOP

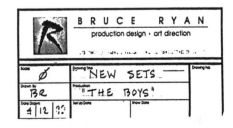

Pencil and graphite stick PERSPECTIVE SKETCH for *The Boys* (Television).

A Last Word

The drafting skills outlined in this book can give you great power as a draftsperson or designer. You have learned that each step along the way must be mastered before going ahead. From making a letter to drawing a line to creating texture, you have again and again encountered primary skills that needed to be perfected.

Only by building on these basic skills will you ever be able to communicate in the drafting vocabulary with precision and integrity. This basic footing will serve you well in any drafting situation, whether it is drawing a floor plan for a community theater production or drafting elevations for the Academy Awards. The most complicated assignment is composed of the most basic steps.

I encourage you to continue to practice your new language as much as you can. As you undertake more and more drafting projects you will find yourself molding a personal drafting style. From the look of your printing to the flair with which you dimension, with practice, your drafting proficiency will only continue to advance. Experience will be your teacher now as you move ahead.

Scenic Design Architectural Standards

Doors

1. standard height = 6'-8"
2. widths:
   3'-0" = exterior to interior entrance
   2'-6" = interior to interior entrance
   2'-2" = closet or bathroom entrance
3. door frame to door clearance:
   $\frac{1}{4}$" = jamb to door
   $\frac{1}{2}$" = header to door
   $\frac{1}{2}$" = sill to door
4. jamb mounting techniques on muslin flats:
   painted trim: mount the jamb (thickness of the reveal) on the back of the flat. Paint the trim.
   dimensional trim: method A: Mount the jamb on the back of the flat. Mount the trim on the front of the flat $\frac{1}{4}$" away from the opening all around.

method B: Door, jamb, and trim will be an independent unit (door casing). The opening in the flat will be larger than if method A was used in order to accommodate the support blocks on this unit.

5. knob height = 3'-0"

Stairs

1. maneuverable angle = 20°–50°
2. safe angle = 30°–35°
3. sum of riser and tread = 17"–18"
4. escape stairs = 6" rise, 11$\frac{1}{4}$" tread
5. onstage rise = 6"–7"
6. onstage tread = 10$\frac{1}{2}$"–11$\frac{1}{4}$"
7. width—one person = 2'-0" minimum
8. width—two people = 3'-0"–3'-6"
9. handrail = 32" or 33" from the tread at the edge of the nosing to the top of the handrail

Index